MEXICAN AMERICAN PRIDE AND HISPANIC UNITY

Filiberto Cavazos, MD

Dorrance Publishing Co
585 Alpha Drive
Pittsburgh, PA 15238
Visit our website at www.dorrancebookstore.com

ISBN: 978-1-6491-3472-1
eISBN: 978-1-6491-3821-7

Mexican American Pride and Hispanic Unity

PROLOGUE

I WAS BORN IN MONTEMORELOS, NUEVO LEON, MEXICO in 1933. My family had moved back from Edinburg, Texas in 1931 after having lived in Texas for more than fifteen years. So, you could say my family has both Mexican and American roots.

My father was quite successful and prosperous in Texas. He was a barber at the time with a shop on one of Edinburg's main streets. It was an attractive, clean establishment, with four classical-style barber chairs and employees to tend them. My parents moved from Montemorelos to Texas in 1915 because the revolution came to town with its violence and they did not feel safe there. Eventually, they brought other members of the family to the Edinburg area and to Reynosa on the Mexican side of the border. Three of my sisters are American born. My eldest sister, like me, was born in Mexico and was brought to Texas as a baby. We have extensive families on both sides of the border. All of them are smart, responsible, outstanding citizens, and I am proud of them.

I regret never asking my father and mother why they went back to Mexico, being as well connected as they were in Texas. Now that I have learned more about the life of Mexican Americans in Texas, I am sure that it was because of the way Mexican people were treated at that time of the Great Depression. My family, being progressive, enterprising, and good citizens found it difficult to accept the prejudice and resentment the Depression brought out in some white Texans. Because I grew up in Mexico, I was able to become a physician, which wouldn't have been possible if we had stayed in Texas. I am happy to report that new generations of the family are mostly professionals, and those who have chosen other paths are also successful in their endeavors.

My life in Mexico was wonderful. Growing up we were not rich, but neither were we poor; our family life was comfortable enough. I was always a dreamer preferring to read and fantasize about my future rather than play with friends, until my father urged me to get out of the house. Montemorelos was a small town when I was growing up. It had a varied ethnic population and we knew everyone. There were old Spanish, Italian, Arab, Jewish, and German families. There were no racial distinctions. The very rich would attend functions of the middle-class families, who formed the majority of the population.

I became a physician, but my first loves as a child were history and geography. When it came time to decide upon a career, it was somewhat difficult for me to choose between medicine and engineering—I liked both. Upon graduation from medical school, I went to West Virginia for my internship and have stayed in the United States since, except for a short medical residence in Brantford, Ontario, Canada. There I had the extraordinary luck of meeting my wonderful wife Carol Anne née Gingrich. Our Canadian family is outstanding and accomplished, and Carol and I are proud of them, as we are of our own extraordinary children.

At the outset, I must remind you I am not a professional historian. Yet I have wanted to write this book for twenty years, and over that time I have been concerned with the disappointed lives and inferior status of Mexican Americans in this country. In a way I am glad I waited, because now I see encouraging developments in the lives of Mexican Americans in this country. Precisely at this time, it is crucial that we transform ourselves and attain the accomplishment and the respect we deserve as a proud race. Let's honor the deep roots we have in the wonderful land that we call America. When reading this book, even though I mention the injustices committed towards our people, I do not want you to dwell on them. Much has been written about the injustices already. What we need to do is to advance beyond them and win recognition and respect from our fellow citizens. So, no more excuses. Let us work on solving our problems. Let us fight together for our redemption.

Let us be proud Mexican Americans. More than that, let us embrace our American heritage and be proud of it.

As you read through this book, you will notice that references to citations are omitted. The thoughts expressed in this book represent years of thinking and collecting information, including reading many well-written and documented books and articles.

This is a short list of sources that informed the writing of this book:

BOOKS:

Arana, Marie. *Silver Sword and Stone: Three Crucibles in the Latin American Story*. New York: Simon and Schuster 2019.

Chipman, Donald E. *Spanish Texas 1591-1821*. Austin TX: University of Texas Press, 1992.

Christensen, Carol and Thomas Christensen. *The U.S.-Mexican War: Companion to the Public Television Series*. San Francisco, CA: Bay Books, 1998.

Corchado, Alfredo. *Homelands: Four Friends, Two Countries, and the Fate of the Great Mexican-American Migration*. New York: Bloomsbury Publishing, 2018.

Flores Caballero, Romeo. *Revolución y Contrarevolución en la Independencia de México*. Mexico, DF Editorial Oceano, 2009.

MacDonald, Lloyd, L. *Tejanos in the 1835 Texas Revolution*. Gretna, LA. Pelican Publishing, 2009.

Matovina, Timothy M. *The Alamo Remembered: Tejano Accounts and Perspectives*. Austin: University of Texas Press 1995.

Montejano, David. *Anglos and Mexicans in the Making of Texas 1836-1986*. Austin: University of Texas Press, 1987.

Muños Martinez, Monica. *The Injustice Never Leaves You: Anti-Mexican Violence in Texas.* Cambridge, MA: Harvard University Press, 2018.

Peña, José Enrique de la. *With Santa Anna in Texas 1807-1841: A Personal Narrative of the Revolution.* Translated and edited by Carmen Perry. College Station, TX: Texas A&M University Press, 1975.

Richardson, Chad. *Batos, Bolillos, Pochos and Pelados: Class and Culture on the South Texas Border.* Austin: University of Texas Press, 1999

Thompson, Jerry. *Cortina: Defending the Mexican Name in Texas.* College Station, TX: Texas A&M University Press, 2007.

Tijerina, Andrés. *Tejanos and Texas under the Mexican Flag 1821-1836.* College Station, TX. Texas A&M University Press, 1994.

OTHER SOURCES FREQUENTLY USED:

Wikipedia

Magazines: *Time Magazine, Texas Monthly.*

Newspapers: *San Antonio Express News, The Monitor* (McAllen TX). *The Wall Street Journal.*

Medical sources: *Journal of the Medical American Association (JAMA), New England Journal of Medicine (NEJM), Archives of Internal Medicine, Archives of Pathology.*

ACKNOWLEDGMENTS:

 I WANT TO THANK MY FAMILY. First of all, my wife Carol, who has been so patient with me. She has tolerated papers and books in the kitchens, on tables and the floors of our houses through the years while I have been collecting information for this book and others planned. She tolerates and sometimes tries to tidy my terribly busy office that combines medical literature, medical and non-medical books, and my manuscripts. Carol has been an inexhaustive source of ideas and inspiration.

I especially thank our niece Jan Horner for her help in editing this manuscript.

I dedicate this book to our children Anne, John, and Paul. They are good kids, hardworking, and dedicated in their occupations. They are Mexican Americans, actually Mexican Canadian Americans. I want them to be challenged by this book. Indeed, I want them to follow in the path I have suggested for all Mexican Americans and be role models themselves. I will challenge them to work, along with all Mexican Americans, on the ideas expressed in this book.

Most of all I dedicate this book to our daughter Karen Elizabeth Cavazos, JD. May she rest in peace. She always loved Mexico, loved Mexican food, Mexican music, and her Mexican family. Karen was so smart that in spite of bipolar disorder affecting her during her studies, she was able to graduate as a lawyer. After graduation, she joined the Chicago Public Defender's Office where she was particularly dedicated in defending Mexican Americans and black Americans abused by the Chicago Police and courts. She is terribly missed in our lives.

MEXICAN AMERICAN PRIDE
Introduction

 THE RESTORATION OF MEXICAN AMERICAN PRIDE is a priority that all those who share this rich heritage must attain. For many years the people of Mexican descent in America have been excluded from the American dream forcibly and by being told of their ethnic inferiority. These factors together with different customs and traits have contributed to their marginalization and a lack of progress in comparison with other national groups that compose the American tapestry.

In order to become the proud group that Mexican Americans richly deserve, they must individually take the steps that follow. We will call these steps: The Mexican American Principles.

1. I will be proud of my Mexican American heritage. At the same time and above all, I will live and be a proud American.

2. I will facilitate, encourage, and demand that my children graduate from high school. I will also encourage them to do their best in order to be able to pursue a college career.

3. I will educate myself as much as possible so I become an informed person.

4. It will be a priority for me and for my family to read, speak, and communicate in English. I will also encourage the retention or learning and practicing of Spanish as a highly useful second language.

5. If I am not now, I will become a United States citizen as soon as possible. I will also encourage friends and relatives to do the same.

6. As a proud and duty-bound American citizen, I will always exercise my voting rights.

7. I will participate in political affairs as a voter and if possible, as a candidate for office.

8. I will always support and protect the rights of Mexican Americans and other Hispanics including those who are undocumented.

9. I will support Mexican Americans and other Hispanics as candidates for public office, but I will demand performance and honesty from them.

10. I will demand respect for my human rights and the rights of all other racial and national groups.

11. I will oppose racial profiling when used for abuse of anyone's rights.

12. I will always provide economic and moral support for members of my family. I will strive to become a role model for them.

13. As a male I will treat all females with respect. As a female I will expect and demand respect from males and other females, while in turn, I will treat everyone with respect.

14. I will work as steadily and as hard as I can in my job or chosen profession, and I will try to advance as high as is possible.

15. I will take care of my health and my family's health, including maintaining healthy eating habits and avoiding unhealthy habits such as smoking, excessive use of alcohol, and use of illegal drugs.

16. I will patronize businesses owned by Mexican Americans and other Hispanics. As a Mexican American business owner, I will do my best to provide service that is honest and of the highest value possible to my clients.

17. I will not use services of businesses, organizations, or enterprises that discriminate against Mexican Americans, Hispanics, minorities or any other national or racial group.

18. I will patronize and support organizations, business, and enterprises that support Mexican American and other Hispanic causes.

19. I will forget the Alamo as a symbol of Anglo supremacy and the source of discriminatory practices against Mexican Americans and Mexican Heritage.

20. As a Mexican American, Hispanic, and Latin American born in the American Continent, I will be prepared to promote and improve relations with the other American Nations with whom we share the Western hemisphere.

In the following chapters, the reason behind each of these principles will be discussed and developed. Possible solutions to problems that Mexican Americans and the United States as a whole face, will also be offered.

Mexico and Latin America offer unending opportunities for the United States economy and security. For far too long the United States has ignored and neglected the nations of the western hemisphere despite promises from several American presidents.

As Mexican Americans together with our Hispanic brothers and sisters, we have the opportunity and duty to make our continent a beacon of progress, freedom, and opportunity for all of us North Americans and South Americans. We need to convert this dream into reality.

Mexican Americans have to become true Americans and be seen as true Americans. We need to change perceptions, old attitudes, and invigorate ourselves to take the responsibility that we owe to our country. In the twenty-first century and beyond, we must keep and sustain American leadership in the world.

MEXICAN AMERICAN PRIDE
PRINCIPLE NUMBER 1

I will be proud and I will honor my Mexican heritage.
At the same time, I will always live and be a proud American.

 IN THIS INITIAL CHAPTER WE WILL DISCUSS THE FOLLOWING:

1. The meaning of Mexican American Pride.

2. Mexican Americans Family traits.

3. Mexican Americans and Mexican Work habits and endurance.

4. Migrant agricultural work conditions, employer's treatment, and public perception about the value of their work.

5. Impact of their need to travel. Impact on the family and their household. Impact on their children's education.

6. The living conditions of migrant workers. Migrant worker's wages and income.

7. The impact of China on the American worker and on the country.

8. Impact of a rising China on the United States.

9. President Trump and his efforts to keep China from emerging as a world power.

10. The North American Free Trade Agreement (NAFTA) now United States-Mexico-Canada Agreement (USMCA) and Latin America.

11. The real value of farmworkers and other menial workers to the American Economy and the difficulty in finding alternatives.

12. The possible way to improve these workers' lives by engaging people and businesses that profit directly from their work.

13. The need to establish an independent group to monitor compliance with reasonable labor rules and living conditions.

14. The need to raise the appreciation of agricultural and other unskilled work in order to enhance Mexican Americans ability to integrate.

15. Discrimination against Mexicans and Mexican Americans and Mexican American Integration.

16. The ambivalent relations between Mexicans in Mexico and Mexican Americans.

17. Mexican Americans in military service. Contributions of Mexicans, Mexico, and Pan-American nations as Allies in World War II.

18. The United States' lack of acknowledgment of the contribution of Latin American nations to the World War II alliance, in contrast with the friendship of the United States with the former enemy nations.

19. The cruel, unjustified deportation of Mexican American veterans after minor offences, many caused by post-traumatic stress disorder.

20. Measures that Mexican Americans must take to put aside the undeserved injustices and offences received and instead concentrate on efforts to better serve the country, now and in the future.

21. Given the bilingual facility and the future increase in population percentage in the United States, Hispanic Americans can help to unlock the potential of our sister nations in Latin America. We can help improve their economy and political stability. At the same time, the United States can benefit by increasing in economic relations and decreasing the need for Latin Americans to migrate. Hopefully we can get ahead of future Chinese incursions in the area.

22. The Mexican American cultural legacy received by Mexican Americans and the opportunities it represents for Mexican American business opportunities and economic improvement.

Mexican American pride does not mean superiority over any other group. Pride in this sense is being comfortable with your heritage, Mexican and American. It means doing the utmost to do as well as any other group of Americans. We must improve our standing economically, educationally, politically, and in every sense socially. Our aim is for Mexican Americans to take the place in American society that most other national groups have attained.

Mexican Americans have strong and supportive family ties. This translates into a very good backup system when needed. In the care of the elderly, the infirm, or the needy, these strong family loyalties offer significant advantages. Respect for the elder family members and the parents and love for the mother are traditional.

Divorce in contrast with other national groups is still relatively low among Mexican Americans. This means more family stability and fewer single-parent homes. Strong family ties also provide family support for the children when disease, divorce, a single-parenting situation, or other circumstances require. That support is also there when both parents have to work.

The capacity of Mexican Americans to work hard in difficult conditions is also traditional and recognized. Mexican Americans work hard at jobs that require patience, endurance and tolerance for adverse conditions. They work at jobs that other groups in this country avoid or refuse.

Most of the migrant agricultural, jobs are performed under adverse circumstances without adequate transportation, housing and personal health facilities. Migrant workers are often mistreated by their employers, poorly paid for their efforts, unappreciated by the consumer who benefits from their work and not infrequently discriminated against by service providers they seek out while away from their home.

While away, migrant workers at times face disastrous situations such as auto accidents or mechanical failure of their transportation conveyance requiring expenditures that they can hardly afford or for which there is no good alternative. They may sustain injuries at work. Injuries for which they may not be treated and certainly not compensated. In addition, while away, migrant workers may face damage or even loss of their property by weather, criminality, or accidental circumstances.

The yearly migration of agricultural workers has severe consequences for the migrant children. The children must interrupt schooling with consequent loss of educational opportunities. They may also be the source of their classmate's ridicule when they must leave before spring for work up north, out west, or simply out to where the agricultural work is needed.

In not a small way this migratory activity contributes to school dropouts. It is truly admirable that migrant children are at times able to overcome these terrible odds and become outstanding members of society and even leaders. It makes you think about the loss to the Mexican American community and to our country. It makes you think about the accomplishments that these individuals could attain if given the proper educational conditions that others enjoy.

It is estimated that there are at least 2,400,000 agricultural workers, many of whom are migrant workers and, in the majority, Mexican Americans. Many of them are undocumented migrants from Mexico and Central America. Few guest agricultural workers are admitted annually under H-2A visas. Lately African workers and workers from the Middle East have replaced Mexican workers, many of whom have gone back to Mexico.

Agricultural federal hourly minimum wage is 7.25 per hour or annually $15,800. Some states such as California have set the minimum hourly pay to $12.00, this equals an annual income of $24,960. A few states such as Georgia set a minimum wage of $5.15 That represents an annual income of $10,712. The nature of farmwork, which is temporary, subject to the work needed at the farm, sometimes layoffs, other times long hours for which overtime is rarely paid. Because of all these variables the agricultural worker annual income is rarely $20,000 and frequently is in the range of $10,000 to $12,000. Most farmworkers fit the definition of living in poverty according to federal poverty guidelines. Construction workers wages are somewhat better with an estimated annual income of $32,000. The income level varies with the state of residency. Unskilled workers in United States earn from $18,000 to $32,000 annually, and Mexican Americans and Hispanics are the main suppliers for low-skilled type of work.

The treatment of migrant workers by some employers is barely humane, and it is worse in some states than in others. Working conditions seem to have improved in California while Texas has the distinction of having some of the worst working conditions for agricultural workers.

Migrant workers and unskilled workers live frequently in areas called Colonias. Colonias are areas develop by unscrupulous landowners who subdivide an area into small lots and sell them at a very low price with easy payments. The price, of course, does not include roads or facilities such as running water drainage, public lighting or electrical service. School buses often have a difficult time reaching the student's home. Some effort has been dedicated to improving the colonias but most still are of primitive construction and lack essential services.

Migrant work under its present conditions must stop. Ideally migrant workers should have local sources of jobs to allow them to stop the yearly disruption of their lives. American industry and manufacturing would greatly benefit if they would take advantage of the high work ethic shown by migratory workers. The United States most assuredly would be better off if these workers were given that opportunity rather than sending the work and technology to China and the rest of Asia.

Certainly, taking advantage of the low wages in China contributes, for the time being, to Americans enjoying cheap prices of goods and American industry enjoying greater profits. But how long will it be before Asian workers demand better pay and before China becomes the second superpower behind the United States and to which our Treasury department is so deeply indebted? China is already the second largest world economy. China has lifted over 850 million Chinese from poverty in the last thirty years.

It would not be a significant loss of profits by American industry if they voluntarily retain half or even a quarter of their manufacturing capacity at home. The savings in transportation costs and the cost of delays, coupled with the relatively low wages that migrant and other workers demand would go a long way to compensate for the lower production costs in Asia. If work was retained at home, it would represent better lives for the American worker. Workers would be better able to afford to maintain the American economy. The United States economy would flourish instead of the stagnation we may face if we continue to export those resources to Asia.

It is said and is patently true that money circulates multiple times in a community and in a nation when it is earned and spent locally. Money goes from the employer to the employee, from the employee to the merchant, from the merchant to provider of services and suppliers, and from here back to the merchant possibly multiple times and eventually to the employers who are themselves consumers. This interplay of money and resources circulating in the nation keeps everyone active and useful to the community.

What happens when all of these resources are exported to other countries and they improve the other countries' economies instead of the United

States economy? CHINA happens and Singapore and the Asian "Tiger" nations happen. Certainly, there are advantages to globalization that cannot be denied. Free trade is for the most part advantageous to the entire world population. What happens, however, when a country has little to export and imports everything instead? It seems that the United States IS this type of country.

Presently our economy is doing well because we Americans are great consumers. The results are plain to see, that is if we are willing to open our minds. Our people went to China initially because we wanted their enormous number of consumers to buy our stuff. What actually happened is that they produced the stuff there, with our own technology and equipment. Then, they bought their own stuff and turned around and sold that same stuff to us. We bought it enthusiastically. Apparently, there is nothing to worry or lose sleep about, our treasury department is already printing the bonds so we can pay for it. We only owe 23 trillion dollars. The Chinese will lend the money back to us at a reasonable interest; they are excellent business people. Thank heavens we have Donald Trump "The Negotiating Genius" on our side.

The problem is extremely serious; it seems that most consumer goods in our stores and sold on the Net are imported from China and Asia. Even some of our food seems to be produced there. First, we exported our jobs to Mexico and Central America and when we found cheaper workers in Asia, we sent those jobs there. We sent everything to China, we sent the technology, we shared the intellectual property (The price to set up shop in China) we sent the machinery, and we trained—actually, our soon to be ex-employees trained the foreign workers that were to replace them.

At least Mexican and Central Americans buy back from the United Sates, but we have considerable difficulty making Asian countries buy what we produce at home. A trade imbalance with China of many billions of dollars annually demonstrates our inability to sell our goods there in spite of the supposedly huge potential market for our products. Every six years our trade deficit with China grows to a trillion dollars and grows over a quarter of a trillion every year. China utilizes those billions and trillions of dollars to buy American government bonds with the consequential potential loss of our economic independence.

American industry and employers must be convinced that the present situation of unilateral trade benefits for Asian countries, (all Asian countries not only China) and negative trade balances for the United States is unsustainable. If something is not done, it will have severe harmful consequences for our nation. President Trump is right in trying to rein in the unfair situation. We need to have a correct and fair trade balance. We need to stop China from illegally raiding our technology and we need China to respect our patents and intellectual property. Above all we need China to open its market to fair competition from our people.

President Trump is also trying to rein in the inevitable rise of China as a world power by preventing our industries from selling China key components for its technological hardware. The object is to stop the expansion of Chinese technology industries in the international markets. He cites security concerns that may be partly right, but such concerns seem self-serving. These blocking steps may be temporarily successful, but Chinese people are very patient and smart. They have been around for at least five thousand years and have overcome worse obstacles. We need to find a way to peaceful co-existence with China. For the time being, what we need is to open their markets to us and stop the unfair trade practices. China has been able to raise its people out of poverty. We need to bring out of poverty and homelessness our own people. China has made great advances in their infrastructure, built large modern cities and made great advances in education and health. China did all of these by putting to work its massive population in manufacturing and commerce. We also need to provide our own with better infrastructure, better educational opportunities and better medical care.

We must find the way to provide manufacturing jobs not only for Mexican Americans but for all our willing workers. We either bring back the work and technology or produce more advanced technology that not only makes the products, but makes better products. Technology advances daily and our people are smart. Let us occupy our people doing great smart things.

We must bring work and technology back to North America. The framework for a much fairer and favorable trade partnership already exists in the form of NAFTA or its successor the USMCA trade deal. This international trade pact has been of great benefit to the people of the United States, Canada, and Mexico.

Mexican Americans and other Hispanic Americans could and should be prepared to play a significant role in promoting and managing trade with the Latin American countries. The United States has more similarity with the American nations than with Asian nations. United States urgently needs to get involved in Latin America before China expands its already significant economic influence there.

In contrast with United States trade with Asia, NAFTA trade has generated a net increase in employment within the United States. The added benefit of trade with Latin American nations is that there is no need for United States security concerns. Latin American countries generally rely on the United States for defense, and they would not be expected to use any economic benefits to increase their military power. Presently there is great concern about China's economic influence in southeastern Asia. Concurrently there is great concern about China's rise in military expenditures and for China's ultimate aim to be top dog in the region. There is an uncanny resemblance of China's aim and the Monroe doctrine and the "Devine Destiny" of the United States in the western hemisphere. It may be appropriate for the United States to recognize that China has enormous and appropriate interest in the region.

There is little hope that the situation of our agricultural workers will improve if something is not done. Bringing about change needs the involvement and cooperation of the public, the employers, and the businesses that buy agricultural and similar products. It is important to include in the group other similar types of workers, from those who work in the fields to those tending the meat packing companies, the chicken industry workers, and other farm jobs.

As Mexican Americans we wish that our people escape menial types of work to have jobs that are better paid and have perceived greater value to society. The truth is that our country cannot get by without the work of these abnegated, abused, and deprecated workers. Their status in society must be improved because no other people and no one else is going to take on this onerous, difficult poorly paid work. Their work and sacrifices must be recognized for what they are: a great contribution to American society and the American economy worth billions and trillions of dollars in economic terms. Their work is too hard and too important and there is no one else to do it. By the way, who is going to build our houses, work in restaurants and do our yard work? Who is going to take care of our children when husband and wife go to work? Most of these jobs are performed by Mexican Americans and Hispanics in most of the country.

What can be done? First and foremost, we, all Americans need to change the way we think about these people. They are human beings and like us, they need to be treated as such. They have feelings, feelings that at times and perhaps frequently are deeper than ours. Some of them suffer alone and away from their families. Some worry if they will have enough money to feed and support their families. Some worry if they will be able to send money back home, some because they depend on the work of their spouse and their children.

The undocumented worker suffers from having to tolerate abuse and low pay. If they protest, they are threatened with calling immigration to have them deported. They fear deportation and having to leave their family behind. The family who they fear to leave behind may include children who are American citizens by birth. They labor to support their loved ones and ultimately, they work to provide food and comforts to the rest of us. Stop thinking of them as invaders, consumer of resources that they are not entitled. Also stop thinking of them as illegal aliens, most of them are not. Stop thinking of them as criminals, most of them behave much better than the average American. Most of them avoid contact with police even though they are more often the victims and because the police are frequently prejudiced against them. Hispanic like black Americans are victims of racial profiling. Trump has done enormous damage to the Mexican Americans. He has called us "Criminals and rapists and sometimes maybe good people." He has inspired white supremacists to take action in defense of the country against the Hispanic "invasion," and he is perhaps unwitting guilty of the killing of Mexican and Mexican Americans in El Paso.

There are other things that can be done to address the injustices. Industries and businesses that benefit from the work that the farmworker and other similar workers do can help. Companies such as Kroger, Walmart, Albertson's, Costco, Publix, HEB, Aldi, Win Co, Sam's Club, Amazon, and others can threaten not to buy products from producers who mistreat their workers or do not pay adequate wages. These retailers could also consider raising payments by a minimal amount to producers who do, as compensation for costs related to compliance. These companies could sponsor a group of inspectors who would review the living conditions and the fairness of the wages they pay to their workers. Many states, including Texas, have inspectors that are supposed to certify compliance with labor laws to that effect. The problem is that such inspections do not work because enforcement is lax and the abuse continues year after year. Reports of violations are rarely corrected or simply accepted after minimal changes are made.

An investigative group sponsored and managed by the grocers and other merchants operating nationally or regionally would be of great help in alleviating the abusive treatments and inhuman conditions with which agricultural workers are treated. The precedent and model already exist in Jerry's Ice Cream refusing to buy milk from producers who would not pay and treat their workers fairly.

A more significant and meaningful solution to the problems that farmworkers and other workers face would be to make undocumented workers eligible to receive Blue Cards. Blue Cards would allow undocumented workers to stay in the country, work without fear of deportation, and would legitimize their residence. Legislation has been introduced both in the House and Senate by members of the California delegation. Blue Cards would provide the protection that Green Cards provide legal immigrants but would have significantly different conditions for their issuing.

The Blue Card program could be part of a new immigration reform proposal that could include a provision for the so-called Dreamers. These two vexing problems, the status of undocumented farmworkers and the status of the American people brought illegally as children need urgent solution because they are the greatest obstacles to the progress of Mexican Americans and other Hispanics in this country.

There is no doubt that as long as there is illegal migration, farmworkers and other workers abuse (construction workers, domestic helpers, etc.) there will not be full integration of Hispanics in the fabric of this country. The lack of integration affects all Hispanics, but Mexican Americans seem to bear the brunt of this marginalization.

The lack of fully recognized integration is related to the problem in how Mexican Americans are perceived. We Mexican Americans have been in the United States close to two hundred years (since Texas was accepted in the Union) and we have been in this land as long as the arrival at Plymouth Rock of English refugees. Yes, many of us were integrated by force, not because we crossed the border but because the border crossed us. We have been integrated since that time but discriminatory and often criminal actions on the part of white Texan settlers maintain the perception that we are not "real" Americans.

We have been Americans from the time that Texas was admitted in the Union in 1845. Californios and New Mexicans were also integrated by force when United States wrestled the western part of the country from Mexico.

Emblematic of the European Americans ignorance of the status of Mexican Americans is the recent writing by one of America's most respected journalists Tom Brokaw. Brokaw had the misfortune of equating integration with homogenization. Integration of Mexican Americans into the United States population is real and present. The problem is that European Americans refuse to recognize it. Homogenization, the act of being like everyone else, will never happen. Our culture, our love for music, our artistry is so authentic that it keeps us from the mediocrity of homogenization. We Mexican Americans and Latin Americans in general are not so unusual in American society. Other groups such as Irish Americans, Italian Americans, Jewish Americans among others have strong roots in their national origin. We celebrate these different identities with happiness and gratitude. Irish Americans celebrate St. Patrick Day and with all other Americans we celebrate that day as well. German Americas celebrate Octoberfest and make the rest of us happy and giddy. Italian Americans celebrate Columbus Day and we celebrate with them the day our unique Latin American race and heritage began. We enjoy and often participate in the celebration of other cultural groups such as those of Greek Americans, Indian Americans, Chinese Americans, and Jewish Americans among others.

Recognition of the value of Mexican Americans and Hispanics to the country is paramount and our efforts and value will be recognized only when the value of the humblest of our group's work is recognized.

There are two distinguished Mexican American among the thinkers and writers in this country. One is Ruben Navarrette whose column appears in daily newspapers. The other is journalist Alfredo Corchado who wrote an enjoyable book called *Homelands*. Navarrette was born in this country; his grandparents came to the United States a long time ago. Corchado was born in Mexico, emigrated with his parents, lived a long time in El Paso, Texas, and became a United States citizen. These two individuals are wonderful representative samples of the Mexican American population. Navarrette calls himself an American Mexican American; Corchado is an ideal representative of what I would call a Mexican Mexican American.

Navarrette, the American Mexican American, does not allow himself to think or act other than as an American. In common with other American Mexican Americans he somewhat resents (not without reason) the way they are treated by Mexico and Mexicans. Corchado is a Mexican Mexican American (like me). He is definitively American but has a soft spot in his heart for Mexico.

Navarrette apparently had been asked to somewhat represent Mexico in the United States, and he flatly refused. He thinks that Mexico only wants him because of the money spent in Mexico as an American tourist. His wife, who was born in Mexico, according to him, has tried to make his heart more considerate towards Mexico, and I, for one, hope that she succeeds. Corchado thinks like I do, that Mexican Americans should be like Jewish Americans and consider Mexico a very close to second to the United States in their hearts and actions. I encourage all Mexican Americans to think like Corchado.

I have said that there is some reason for Navarrette's attitude towards Mexico and Mexicans. There are several things that Mexico and Mexicans should and must do to have a rapprochement. First of all, Mexicans and Mexico must recognize that Mexican Americans are truly Americans, and they should not expect their Spanish to come easily if at all. Some Mexican Americans have never spoken Spanish. If they try to practice their Spanish on you, be pleased for that, and help them, do not criticize or laugh at their efforts. My own kids by the present definition are American Mexican Canadian. They love Mexico almost as much as I do but hardly utter a word of Spanish, though they try. One of my girls loved Mexico so much. She loved to visit Mexico. Many times, she introduced me to lovely Mexican music.

But whatever we are: American Mexican Americans, Mexican Mexican Americans, or whatever other combination of Mexican and Americans there is; whatever our degree of success in pursuit of the American dream, we have work to do. The list is long. One of the most important is to lift the appreciation and recognition of the work that agricultural and other humble Mexican Americans do, for only by lifting them will the rest of us be elevated to the place we Mexican Americans deserve.

Another important source of Mexican American pride is our patriotism and loyalty to the United States of America. This is a fact usually dismissed by those who vilify Mexican Americans and who ignore the fact that Mexican Americans serve in the United States military in greater proportion than the Mexican American population in the country.

Mexican Americans have participated in every conflict that the United States has been involved particularly since the Second World War. During the Second World War an estimated 500,000 and 750,000 Mexican Americans participated in the armed forces. Those figures include American Mexican Americans (those born in the United States) and Mexican Mexican Americans (those actually born in Mexico).

Both groups participated enthusiastically in fighting against the Axis powers and their wish for world domination. The enthusiasm of Mexican Mexican Americans was partly due to the promise they would be granted American citizenship if they served in the armed forces. At the time, there was apparently sincere but unfortunately, outright propaganda exalting the unity of all the American nations. That was to imply the inclusion of Latin America in the war effort as an ally to the United States and the European Nations.

In movie theaters, at the end of each movie for example there were written statements that said: "Las Americans Unidas, Unidas Venceran." Translated: "The Americas, united, united will be victorious." There were songs sung in the schools that said "immortal America, fountain of light, fountain of liberty," and all Mexicans along perhaps with most Latin Americans believed that we were talking about North America and South America and all our American nations.

At the end of the war we all finally realized that unknown to us, the America that we were singing about was the United States of America because even up to this date there is no mention that most of the Latin American nations declared war against the Axis nations, and because there is no inclusion of Latin American nations as allies of the United States anywhere. By the way, Latin American nations still call themselves Americans. Reserve the name America for the whole continent and call the United States: "United States" not "America." Actually, Canadians also do not call United States "America" but popularly shorten the name and refer to the United States as "The States."

American nations realize that the United States has appropriated itself the name America as part of the "Monroe Doctrine" and the American belief in the "Manifest Destiny." The God-given right for the United States to be the master of the western hemisphere. In any case after the end of the war and ever since, the nations the United States refers to as allies and friends include those in Europe and include the former axis powers Germany, Italy, and Japan. It seems that soon former enemies like Vietnam and North Korea will soon be included in this select group. Interesting is the fact that Cuba, who was an ally in those dark days, continues to be treated as an enemy with the support of the now-aging Cuban Americans. Let's hope that young Cuban Americans will be more charitable to the Cubans remaining in the island nation.

The participation of Latin American nations in the Second World War was mostly economical, providing necessary materials for the war effort. They also provided human resources to replace the workforce that had to be mobilized to increase recruitment of men and women into the armed forces. Increased human resources were also provided for the needed military industrial expansion. Throughout the continent there was also rationing of basic food resources such as corn, sugar, flour, and oils as they were needed for export to the United States who in turn needed those food items for support of the troops.

The required human resources included farmworkers in a program established as the Bracero Program. The Bracero Program was terminated after many years in part due to violations in the conditions provided to the workers. The ending of the Bracero Program did not end the need for farmworkers, and only worsened the conditions of work, the living conditions, pay, and abuse of farmworkers. The farm owners then turned to undocumented Mexican immigrants and later to other groups such as undocumented Central Americans and later yet to African immigrants and immigrants from the Middle East.

There was actual but limited involvement of Latin American troops. Mexico sent a squadron of flyers that saw action in the Pacific flying from the Philippines. The squadron suffered several casualties. Brazil sent a regiment to the European war theater.

Whereas there is a reliable number of Mexican American participants in the Second World War there is no definite number of Mexican Americans in the wars that followed: Korea, Vietnam, Iraq, Afghanistan and minor conflicts. That is because the Mexican American members were no longer counted separately, and in fact there were no records of national origin kept after the Second World War.

Nevertheless, in all of those war efforts there was and continue to be heavy involvement of Mexican Americans serving with distinction and pride in the armed forces.

Equal to the mistreatment of American nations by the United States has been the mistreatment and benign neglect of Mexican American veterans. At times the neglect has been not benign at all but downright cruel such as the deportation of Mexican Mexican Americans and even American Mexican American Veterans suffering from post-traumatic stress disorder or for committing minor offenses. Oftentimes the deportees are Mexican Mexican Americans who were promised American citizenship but did not follow up on requesting that citizenship. The abandonment of veterans who served the country with honor, risking their lives and well-being is shameful. This disgraceful situation could be corrected easily but seemingly people who should care do not seem to act. This is another failure of the promised veterans care. A "Thank You for Your Service" is not at all enough.

Another shameful situation is the treatment of young Mexican American citizens who are deported to Mexico when they have grown up in the United States. These children and young adults are unfamiliar with the life in Mexico. They are lost to the United States and lost to Mexico. There must be a way to salvage these young people. They must be identified, educated in United States or in Mexico. Our countries cannot afford to lose the treasure they represent going to waste.

Talking about the injustices committed and continue to be committed against Mexican Americans in this country is difficult, painful, but necessary. However, taking remedial actions to elevate the bruised self-esteem and the conditions of Mexican Americans is much more necessary. The measures that need to be taken depend mainly and for the most part on the efforts of all of us Mexican Americans. Much hard work was done by veterans returning from the Second World War who refused to go back to the awful prewar conditions after fighting for their country. Much was done to restore human dignity by black leaders and by visionary Mexican Americans. However much more remains to be done. We have to do it for ourselves and for this country that needs the efforts of all Americans to face the challenges of the future.

The United States must re-focus on the needs of its citizens. It needs to improve the lives of individual Americans. There was a time when the

United States rescued the European nations from the disaster of the Second World War with its Marshall plan. Now those nations provide their citizens with excellent transportation systems, educational opportunities, and health services, all seemingly superior to those presently enjoyed by our people. The rest of the world seem to be doing well. Asians do not really need us. Africans are doing better; in any case they are not doing worse than Central American northern triangle countries. Europeans are doing quite well. In our hemisphere we could help many countries and in helping them we could benefit mightily ourselves. Do not let the Chinese do as they did in Panama. Panama was our protectorate; we wrestled it away from Colombia when we built the Panama Canal. We kept the Panama Canal for nearly 100 years. But Panama did not improve as a nation until the Chinese took over and now it is very successful nation. Now China has said it is flirting with Chile and Brazil, and an increasing number of South American nations to extend the Road and Belt Project. Recent commercial pact with Brazil strengthened their friendly relations.

Mexican Americans and our brothers and sisters, other Hispanics are pretty close to majority in majority minority areas of the United States in the near future. Given our Spanish as a second language and our common cultural background, we are in the best position to promote our Latin American nations. There is a huge potential in resources and people in these countries, but they also need our skills and drive to create successful nations. Then those successful nations will be able to consume our products and provide us with theirs. Commercial relations with Latin Americans will be fairer and more beneficial than relations with other continents. Just remember the Mexican belief and saying "After God the Americans" this time meaning "The United States of America."

Certainly, we have no time to lose. We cannot resort to recriminations of the past. There is much we Mexican Americans must do and can do for this, our country and for the improvement of our Mexican American and Hispanic people.

We Mexican Americans share and are the recipients of a great cultural legacy that spans many centuries. This involves and blends centuries of

Latin, European, Moorish, and Jewish cultures with American Indigenous art and culture. This is an enormous cultural inheritance that has been only partially transferred and partially enriched the full American experience. Still there are areas of our Mexican legacy yet to be explored and waiting to be utilized.

By the time Columbus arrived in America, there were advanced indigenous civilizations in what now is Mexico. Remarkable among them were the Aztec and Maya. The Maya civilization is known for its advanced knowledge of the sciences particularly mathematics and astronomy. The Aztecs were powerful warriors who dominated the surrounding tribes and conquered an empire that reached from the Gulf of Mexico to the Pacific Ocean. Both of these cultures built large cities. Tenochtitlan, the Aztec capital was in fact larger in area and population than most capital cities in Europe at the time.

The Spanish that arrived with Hernan Cortez defeated the Aztecs with the help of Aztec rival tribes and gradually took over the entire territory of what is now Mexico and Central America. One of the Spanish objectives was to become rich with the gold and silver found abundantly in Mexico. The other great objective was to spread the Roman Catholic Religion. The priests and missionaries educated the Indians in religion and acted as their protectors. Individual Spaniards were granted lands and were put in charge of the Indians living within the granted lands.

Spanish soldiers and the many civilians that migrated to New Spain, now Mexico, established many cities in central Mexico. Most of the early Mexican cities were located in the vicinity of mines where silver and gold were extracted. Other cities and smaller population centers were centers of commerce or agriculture. Arts and sciences began to flourish in New Spain and the first university was opened in Mexico City in the year 1521.

The evolution of Mexican cuisine started when Spanish explorers made contact with the Mayans. This was followed by a major event: the meeting of Cortez the Spanish Conquistador with Moctezuma the penultimate Aztec King. This the most important event for the history of America and the world is that two rich cultures met, the Latin, Spanish richly varied culture enriched by centuries of Moorish domination and the Mexican Indigenous culture. Not only was the race that we Mexican Americans share born at that propitious time, but two huge cultures fused in a glorious mixture. It was an extraordinary event with no precedent in the history of the world and forever unique.

The original, Indian Mexican cuisine was basically vegetarian, with use of corn, beans of huge variety, herbs, chilies, pumpkins, gourds, sweet potatoes, avocados, nopal, pineapples, guavas, tomatoes, and many other fruits. Cacao and vanilla, world staples were found in Mexico. Here were also innumerable herbs many with medicinal properties whose application in the United States remain largely unexplored. This bounty of food items was augmented with the imports of the old world. Spices and meats, chickens, goats, sheep, pigs, cattle were added to turkeys, ducks, and small mammals, fish and other indigenous sources of animal meats. Use of all these foods are variable throughout Mexico, creating regional types of cuisine that are fun to explore. Of course, tamales, tacos, and enchiladas are widely available throughout Mexico with regional variations.

The French influence in Mexican cuisine took place during the French intervention in Mexico (1861-1867) Maximillian and Carlotta were not completely happy with the food available to them and sent for European chefs who taught Mexicans much, particularly in bread and pastel making. French bakers, by teaching Mexican bakers their craft, transformed existing bread making into an art form that became the Mexican Panaderia. Mexican Panaderia is an art in itself, always worth a visit.

Religious orders in convents were the incubators of great innovations in Mexican cuisine. The inventions included great combinations of chocolate and chilies to produce varieties of sauces; among them are the moles, an incomparable culinary experience.

Some of these foods have been introduced in the United States and are the basis of Tex-Mex and Mexican restaurants. There are also industrial types of production of food of Mexican origin. Some of the original Mexican food items with great success as American food products include

Fritos, the basis of Frito Lay. In Mexico, Fritos in the early 1900s were and still are cylindrical stick-like pieces of fried corn. Tacos have been industrialized and are the success of Taco Bell, Taco Cabana, and others. Store shelves in supermarkets contain numerous American-made products that are adaptations of original Mexican food items. Entrepreneurs, hopefully Mexican Americans, should realize there is still an enormous variety of possible sources of commercial exploitation in the Mexican cuisine.

The Mexican Cuisine has definitely made inroads in American television. Several well-known chefs have regular programs presenting important aspects of the Mexican cuisine along with interesting aspects of Mexican culture.

Mexican American and Tex-Mex restaurants are found throughout the United States Many are owned and run by Mexican Americans; others are run by non-Mexican Americans. There are several chains of Mexican restaurants varying in quality and authenticity. In areas of high Mexican American and Hispanic populations there are restaurants of very good quality and authenticity. The variety of Mexican cuisine is expressed in the wide choice of Mexican restaurants. Some of them are comparable in quality to the better restaurants in Mexico City. There are still opportunities for enterprising Mexican Americans to operate world-class Mexican restaurants in the United States.

The Germans introduced beer in Mexico around 1890 creating very respectable beers, most of them known all over the world and now commercialized by multinationals. Many of these are American. Tequila remains mostly Mexican owned and sold internationally. Other alcoholic beverages are sporadically imported from Mexico. Sotol a form of aguardiente has recently been imported from Oaxaca. Aguardiente, at times sold with the worm in the bottle is manufactured in several Mexican states. Other Mexican alcoholic drinks, such as Tepache—the original Mexican alcoholic sinful drink that sunk the Toltec Empire—remains a local alcoholic drink in central Mexico.

The wine industry began in Mexico in the sixteenth century in what is now the American state California and was mostly associated with the

Catholic Missions. Within Mexico and before Mexican independence, the manufacture of wine, even for religious purposes, was prohibited by the Spanish authorities and had to be imported from Spain. After independence, an important wine industry developed in several Mexican states including Aguascalientes, Coahuila California Norte, and California Sur. The wine produced in Mexico is respectable but has not made its way to the United States. Is it waiting for some Mexican American entrepreneurs?

The variety of the Mexican cuisine is astonishing. It seems that each of the thirty-two Mexican states has its own unique cuisine. As varied as the Mexican cuisine is, so are the arts and crafts of Mexico. The use of materials and colors is infinite and truly defies description. All kinds of artistic expression and media are used. Some of the arts and crafts demand incredible amount of time and great skill to produce. Every time you visit a Mexican market or an artisanal, you find a new artist or new kind of art work. Mexican Americans in this country may be able to trace their family origin to some particular area of Mexico or to a certain Mexican state. In the spirit of enterprise, it would be interesting and profitable to dedicate some effort to acquire and maybe perfect a particular skill or craft of that area. That craft could be the beginning of a highly profitable business in the United States.

When Spaniards made initial contact with the indigenous Mexicans and their art, they attempted to destroy it, thinking the art had a religious meaning. This was contrary to their Catholic belief. The art survived however only to be deprecated by the dictator Porfirio Diaz who tried to impart the art a French flair in his effort to modernize the country. After he was deposed the art resurged with strong impetus and flourished becoming to what today is a wonderful mixture of European and multi-regional indigenous art.

Music for Mexican Americans and for all Latin Americans is a very special blend, enriched by the contributions of every Latin country on earth. We enjoy the music of every nation and make it our own. It is impossible to explain the feelings that music evokes for every Mexican American.

MEXICAN AMERICAN PRIDE
PRINCIPLE NUMBER 2

> I will facilitate, encourage, and demand that my children graduate from high school, and I will encourage them to do their best in order to be able to pursue a college career.

 ISSUES TO BE DISCUSSED UNDER THIS CHAPTER:

1. In the last few years there has been significant improvement in the educational attainment of Mexican Americans; however, there is much more improvement needed to reach the graduation rates of white non-Hispanic and Asian groups.

2. The consequences of low standing in educational attainment are readily apparent when the important issues in American success stories are examined.

3. Criminality in poor areas where Hispanics and Mexican Americans most frequently live, is a negative factor in educational achievement.

4. Historically, Anglos have discriminated against Mexican Americans and held them in low esteem. Mexican and Mexican Americans were easily dispossessed of the lands they owned by many means. The means used included terror, lynching, murder, and illegal means with the complicity of police and governmental entities. The mistreatment of Mexicans

and Mexican Americans occurred throughout the Southwest in the land taken away from Mexico.

5. Integration of Mexican Americans into the fabric of the country requires that Mexican Americans act and feel as Americans living in their own country. This is no different than European immigration.

6. The low esteem Mexican Americans are held in, is exacerbated by the fact that farmworkers and unskilled laborers are in the greater numbers Mexican, Mexican Americans, and Hispanics. For some reason all of these workers are perceived to be Mexican Americans.

7. The work of farmworkers and unskilled workers is essential and extremely important for the nation. The value of their work must be recognized and their income, living conditions, and social status must be improved.

8. For over one hundred years, Mexican Americans underwent discrimination and poor education, attending grossly inadequate and deficient schools. There was also a mindset that Mexican Americans needed only a few years of school because "there was no need to educate Mexicans since they were only going to do peon work."

9. Many factors play a role in the low standing of some schools serving Mexican American students; the greatest factor is that often those schools are located in impoverished areas.

10. To make meaningful changes in Mexican Americans and Hispanic education, parents need to become more interested and involved in Parent-Teacher associations (PTA). Parents must be more aware of the function of School Districts and the importance of electing knowledgeable Board Members.

11. Education opportunities for Mexican Americans are improving practically daily. Mexican Americans are taking the opportunities offered, and if continued, soon we will be talking about the Mexican American success story.

12. As compensation for the many years of mistreatment, it would be a matter of justice if a college system for adults who suffered through those years could be established.

13. The criminal justice system, police methods, and policing must be reformed to discontinue the present bias against Mexican Americans and other minorities.

There has been significant improvement in the educational achievements of Mexican Americans. However, there is still a gap in educational achievement compared with non-Hispanic whites and Asians. Mexican American students still have a high dropout rate compared to other ethnic and national groups. They also rank low in academic achievement testing. These facts have serious consequences for their future social, cultural, and economic development and for their life accomplishments.

Educational achievement statistics are difficult to obtain because more often than not, statistics are combined with figures for the entire Hispanic population. In the professional and financial fields, the impact of lower educational accomplishments is readily apparent. Although Mexican Americans are approximately 12% of the American population, they only account for less than 5% of American physicians. Similar figures can be quoted for the entire healthcare field, including nursing and medical technology. In engineering, science, and technology the figures are just as dismal. There is hardly any mention of Mexican Americans in the financial world. In other words, the education of Mexican Americans is a serious problem that permeates through the entire population and affects not only Mexican Americans but in fact impacts the whole nation.

Mexican Americans are disproportionately represented among the jailed population. Rates for crime including drug-related crimes, gang activity, robbery, and murder are high. This is an unspeakable tragedy and direct consequence of the social and economic environment in which Mexican American children are born and raised. It is also a consequence of the still poor educational environment. Poverty, education issues, and criminality are closely tied.

Mexican American families are economically disadvantaged. Their family income ranks as one of the lowest in America. They often require public assistance and are, compared to other groups, disproportionately higher users of social services.

There are multiple reasons for the low educational achievements of Mexican Americans as a group. Solutions to remedy poorer scholastic achievement are complex and likely to require long and difficult steps.

A large part of the problem is the low self-esteem of Mexican Americans. For over a hundred years first, they were cheated and dispossessed of the lands that were supposed to be theirs to keep as part of the 1848 Guadalupe Hidalgo treaty that gave the United States possession of half of Mexico territory. In addition, they were generally, deprived of the freedom to work in fields other than agriculture and then only as peons, working under Anglo bosses and masters. In agricultural work, as full-time or part-time employees or as sharecroppers they were frequently abused, poorly paid, or cheated of their earnings by numerous strategies. These strategies frequently involved governmental institutions, such as taxing authorities, illegal grand juries, police, and immigration authorities. Even today in many of the occupations in the United States, the lower ranking employees are of Mexican origin while the bosses or higher-ranking employees are Anglo. This undeniably, is at least in part due to discriminatory practices and in part due to Mexican Americans low self-esteem. The low self-esteem is a result of years of discriminatory treatment and the difficulty Mexican Americans have being considered a key part of American society. For Anglos, Mexican Americans will always be Mexican while Anglos are the true Americans. This perception will continue to affect the status of Mexican Americans until this country recognizes the contributions of Mexican Americans.

Mexican American integration will only be fully achieved when all Mexican Americans begin to consider themselves Americans or Americans of Mexican descent rather than Mexicans living in the United States. Integration will happen when Mexican Americans have a better opinion of themselves, and they participate in this country as American citizens. It will happen when Mexican Americans have pride in themselves and realize that Anglos are not superior, more intelligent, or more able, but are people who have been brought up in an English only speaking environment, confident of who they are, which makes it easier for Anglos to succeed in this country. Full integration in American life does not mean renunciation of their Mexican heritage or abandoning cultural traits that make Mexican Americans' lives meaningful and unique. Every American is in essence an immigrant in this country or a descendant of one. Mexican Americans are no different except that many Mexican Americans became Americans when the borders changed. What integration means is full participation as American citizens. In fact, it is essential that all Mexican Americans fulfill the principles expressed in this book.

One additional factor that encourages discrimination is the willingness of Mexican Americans to perform work that in similar conditions Anglos would not. The willingness to work at these difficult and lower rewarded jobs, perpetuates a low appreciation of the Mexican Americans abilities and creates a subservient status. This willingness to sacrifice, to do a job which others refuse to do, should be recognized as a valuable asset. For the country, their work means billions and trillions of dollars in economic activity. This is the same spirit of sacrifice that Mexican Americans and other Hispanics have, is the same quality that makes good soldiers. It explains why as a group they performed with unequal heroism in America's wars while in particular during the Vietnam War many European Americans chose to avoid military service. This heroism, predictably, was not sufficiently rewarded with medals as was the case in previous conflicts.

It is extremely important for all of us Mexican Americans to recognize the value of the work that agricultural workers perform and do whatever we can to bring them recognition and well-deserved respect. Similar recognition should be given to those who labor in the construction industry and in seemingly menial work. The jobs those humble abnegated people do, allows the rest of us to enjoy a more productive and fulfilling life.

For years, schools serving the Mexican American population were less well provided with the required facilities, equipment, and supplies and they lacked highly qualified, well compensated teachers. Presently the situation is a great improvement over the conditions that were in existence up to the end of the first half of the twentieth century. Earlier, after the Mexican war, Anglos considered education for Mexican American unnecessary. Anglos questioned the need to spend resources to educate people who were destined to do peon work in the fields. Later, schools for Mexican Americans were separate from those of Anglo students. At that time, schools for Mexican American students were mere shacks in comparison to Anglo schools. Mexican and Mexican American parents wishing and able to afford more adequate schooling for their children, had to send them to private, generally, Catholic schools. The situation began to change at the end of the Second World War when Mexican Americans became more assertive about their rights, but inequality still persists in many areas.

Many factors influence and play a role in the low standing of some schools serving predominantly Mexican American populations even today. Inferiority of schools in Mexican American areas is now related mostly to the fact that they are located in poor counties with low tax revenue, upon which school systems depend. Parent-teacher associations in these Mexican American schools are less active and the school curricula are less diversified and demanding. Bilingual education, although controversial, is essential in the early school years for children raised in homes where Spanish is the exclusive means of communication.

Participation in parent-teacher associations (PTA) is much more important than parents of students realize. One of the best things that parents of a Mexican American and Hispanic student can do for the child's success in life is to participate in his or her school PTA. Participation in PTA allows parents to be informed of the direction of school activities and curriculum. PTA participation offers the opportunity to discuss any school-related issue and the opportunity to participate in needed changes. Volunteering in PTA can give a parent a better way to help the student succeed in school and give guidance to career direction and choice. The more a parent participates in PTA activities the greater the child's success. Attending parent-teacher meetings gives parents information about the student's progress and degree of scholastic success. Parent- teacher meetings also inform the degree of the student's adjustment to school activities and information about any further actions needed to optimize the student's school performance.

Another organization of great important for the success of the schools and students is the School Board for the school district of residence. In the United States, public education from pre-kindergarten through high school is governed and administered by district school boards. District school boards have taxing power independent of government structures. Members of school boards are elected officials. It is extremely important for the public to be aware of the knowledge and the ethical principles of the board members for best voting selection. The school districts receive state funding commensurate with the relative state economic resources. The greatest source of economic support for the school district is local estate taxes. These sources of income for the district determine that there are rich school districts and poor school districts. The ability of the school board to provide good teachers, good schools, good programs, and good support for the individual student depends on their available resources. The wealthiest school districts can provide better support for the individual student. Some of the school districts can supply students with personal computers that enhance the learning experience for students who could not otherwise have access to internet services. Many, if not most school districts also provide adult education courses. Adult education in school districts is an important service for Mexican Americans and Hispanics who can learn new skills or even new occupations. Thus, adult education could provide new means of support allowing improved economic status. Some school districts make arrangements with technical colleges to provide well-structured learning experiences.

One important factor in poor scholastic performance is the impression that Mexican American parents do not emphasize education as a priority in child-rearing. This attitude has changed but still is lacking in comparison with other racial and national groups. Mexican American parental attitude towards education is still low compared to the attitude of non-Hispanic white parents and particularly lower than those of Asian parents. Compared with ten years ago Mexican American parents and students in an increasing percentage now consider education important and graduating from high school also very important. The latest available statistics show a definite improvement in high school graduation rates but still lower than non-Hispanic white students' graduation rate of 84.3%. It is anticipated that with the increased interest in college education, parents, and students now the Hispanic and Mexican American high school graduation rate will be as high as those of the white non-Hispanics. College attendance and graduation are similarly anticipated to improve.

Changing parental and student attitudes is challenging and can no longer be blamed on the discriminatory attitudes of Anglos. Other minority, ethnic, and national groups such as Asian students including, Chinese, Indian, Korean, Vietnamese, and other recent arrivals, exceed the graduation rates of non-Hispanic whites. The Asian groups also exceed the rates of graduation of non-Hispanic whites from college and professional schools. Given the appropriate conditions, Mexican American students can compete with any other group in scholastic performance. Today the student population, particularly in states and cities with large Mexican American populations, is predominantly Mexican American. The ability to perform is well demonstrated by the fact than in a recent 2007 study of the best 100 high schools in the United States four were located in poor Mexican American districts in Texas. In south Texas there is a group of schools (South TX ISD) with innovative curricula that makes it possible for nearly 100% of their students to receive college acceptance. Also, in south and central Texas there is a large group of over 120 pre-kindergarten to grade-12 public schools (the IDEA schools) where 100% of their seniors are accepted to four-year colleges. The IDEA schools were named America's best charter

School Network in 2016. These reports give great hopes that with some effort, the situation of Mexican Americans can change in a not-too-distant future. Every effort should be made for this to happen. The Rio Grande Valley and Texas scholastic achievements are great examples of the fact that Mexican Americans can succeed in education. College education was once a distant aspiration for the Rio Grande Valley students. Today it is heartwarming to see the great number of these students partaking in volunteer activities with the idea of increasing their chances to go on to higher education. Now many students take advanced college courses while at high school and some even graduate high school simultaneously with a minor college degree.

In the Rio Grande Valley, much emphasis is now being placed on STEM (Science, Technology, Engineering, and Mathematics) sciences. Here there are also great technical colleges successful in training students for STEM careers. In addition, the Rio Grande Valley has new nursing schools, medical support-oriented training schools, and at least two new universities, including a new Medical School branch of the University of Texas, the Rio Grande Valley Medical School. In El Paso, Texas a new medical school opened in 2016. These two medical schools have a high percentage of Mexican American and Hispanic students raising the hope that one day the needs of Mexican American patients will be satisfied by nurses and doctors of their own cultural background. This will also increase the percentage of Mexican American physicians, more in line with the percentage of Mexican American population. Hopefully what is happening in the Rio Grande Valley of Texas can be repeated in other areas of high Mexican American population.

Community colleges are an important source of accessible college education. Community colleges can also be an important stepping stone in the way to a four-year college education. There are promises to make college education more accessible and freer to qualifying students. One example of such a community college is the multiple campus Alamo College in San Antonio, Texas. With the help of community charitable donors, the college is anticipating it can make good on its promise of free tuition. California, Maryland, New York, Rhode Island, Oregon, Tennessee, and other states offer community college attendance assistance and tuition free to students under certain qualifying conditions.

Significant gains in Mexican American graduation rates and decreases in high school dropout rates is occurring in California—the other state with the highest Mexican American population. Competition for college slots is extremely high in this state with its high percentage of Asian population. Asian parents are generally of a high economic status and have high expectations of their children to succeed and are greatly motivating for their children to succeed. This is almost a complete reversal of the past Mexican American parental attitude. The Asian American students even challenge non-Hispanic whites. As Mexican Americans the challenge posed by the dedication of Asian students must be understood as a welcome opportunity to improve ourselves. We definitively have to change and we can. We need desperately to make our Mexican American parents and students more responsive to this challenge.

A path for increasing the ability of Mexican Americans to attend college exists in Texas where the upper 10% of the graduating class in any high school are guaranteed acceptance in college. This in part, evens the playing field for graduates of "better" and "poorer" schools in terms of the opportunity to attend college. It does not however, make it easier for students of "poor" schools to perform once in college at the same level as the graduates of "better" schools. Remedial opportunities have to be provided for graduates of deficient schools to enable them to have successful college careers. The Texas legislation does not mean equal opportunity for all students regardless of their background, since socioeconomic factors affecting the ability to attend college stand in the way. One of the largest obstacles for Mexican Americans is affordability, since their households, more often than not, lack adequate economic means. The deplorable reluctance of Mexican American parents to send their children to far away colleges, particularly if they are girls is another obstacle. Appreciation of the significant advantage that college attendance and graduation represent for the future of the individual has to be emphasized to reluctant Mexican American parents by any means, particularly by school authorities and by recruiting colleges. Mexican American parents in Texas must take advantage of the opportunity for their children to attend college, even if it means greater sacrifices on their part. Mexican American and Hispanic leaders must work for legislation similar to Texas legislation where at least the upper 10% of any high school is guaranteed college placement opportunity in states where significant Hispanic population exists.

Unfortunately, college expenses are too high for students to afford and for parents to provide. There is no question that American universities are of the highest quality, but the corollary is that their cost is a problem particularly for poor families. There should be better teaching methods using media, artificial intelligence and modern ways of delivering knowledge. This seems to be another subject but making college education affordable is of paramount importance and so essential for American students to be able to compete. When engineers and physicians study in other countries, they obtain their degrees cheaply, practically at no cost and come to this country to compete with physicians and scientists that owe 100,000 dollars or more upon graduation. This situation is not fair for the American graduate and for our country.

There is no question that higher education in the United States is of recognized quality. China and other countries try to send as many students to our universities as they can or as many as the United States government allows. Chinese and other Asian parents in the United States give priority to getting their children accepted into the best universities and colleges they can. Chinese, Indian and other Asian parents both residents in this country and foreigners push their children to perform as well as they can in school. Their objective is to maximize their access to college education. These parents send their children to school to learn. American and Mexican American parents also send their children to learn but also regrettably, to play. Americans and American schools seem to place great importance in school sports. Football is a favorite as anyone can tell with the popularity of "Friday Night Football" on television programs. Schools serving Mexican American students should consider changing the emphasis of their programs to study rather than to sports. Few Mexican Americans seem to play in college football teams and fewer yet advance to play in the NFL. No Mexican American basketball player seems to reach college basketball and no Mexican American plays in the NBA.

Perhaps it is time for those who can, to seek education at foreign colleges and universities at a reasonable cost. In this regard Mexican Americans potentially have the big advantage of going next door to Mexico for training. Mexico has some of the most prestigious universities and technological colleges in Latin America. Apparently, Mexico admits central and South American students at their public universities with little or no difference in fees. Perhaps it is time to find out if Mexico would accept their Mexican American neighbors as well. Of course, safety in Mexico is an issue. Maybe the United States consular services in Mexico could be of help in this regard. Canadian universities are another possibility for Mexican Americans able to afford the cost. Canadian colleges and universities offer low fees to poor Canadian students but for foreign students studying in Canada fees are not necessarily more affordable than in the United States.

In the last several years several universities, including some of the most prestigious have lowered fees for students of low-income families. Some of these institutions charge no fees for families whose income is less than 65,000 dollars a year. Other colleges charge reduced fees for families with incomes up to 125,000 dollars. In addition, a large group of colleges have been designated HSI (Hispanic Serving Institution) indicating teaching institution serving a high percentage (25% of higher) Hispanic students. These universities and colleges receive additional federal funds and actively seek Hispanic students. Many HIS institutions offer facilities and help to make education affordable.

A new university system devised for adult Mexican Americans is proposed as an important step to improve the participation of Mexican Americans in the economic and social life of this country. Through 150 years of virtual slavery. Anglos have done damage to Mexican American lives with impunity and with the encouragement, approval, and support on the part of the local, county, state, and federal governments. This damage now should be alleviated by compensatory measures. Part of this compensation should be by facilitating the establishment and acceptance of university systems for adult Mexican Americans that would allow the accelerated participation of Mexican Americans in professional careers.

These universities and colleges will recruit mature, highly motivated, although scholastically challenged students and adults who wish to pursue college studies. This university system must include highly professional schools in the medical fields, science, engineering, technology, mathematics, and business administration. Features of this system must be: remedial courses to repair scholastic deficiencies, high dependence in audiovisual instructions, media and artificial intelligence, teaching centered in practical, clinical type of issues. The operation of this new system would depend on low fees and guaranteed low-interest student loans. The envisioned Mexican American university system is entirely feasible with some initial help, since it could be self-sustaining with loan paybacks. The paybacks in the proposed university systems would not be nearly as onerous as those incurred by university graduates elsewhere in the United States.

These compensatory measures could be considered comparable with the "reparations" being contemplated for African Americans as compensation for years of slavery, for the theft of lands assigned to them when freed, and for the additional 150 years of discrimination and virtual apartheid These reparations make sense in the present days. Nothing can really compensate for the black American years of slavery and suffering. While touching on this subject of compensation, it is high time that we think about the suffering and the loses of the American Indigenous people who are still living on reservations.

The many factors causing poor scholastic performance of Mexican Americans are additive. Low socioeconomic status of the Mexican American population translates into poverty. Poverty in school districts serving Mexican American students means reduced tax revenues that is insufficient to support adequate schools. Inadequate schools cause poor scholastic performance that eventually translates in low socioeconomic status. This vicious circle needs to be broken and the key lies in finding answers to the various educational challenges. Teachers and parents together with legislators must find ways to increase school funds. One such mechanism is revenue sharing between rich and poor school districts. This mechanism should be temporary to allow for a raise in the economy of Mexican American areas and school districts. A preferred mechanism would be a greater share of state and federal revenues to go to all schools, particularly to schools in poor districts.

THE CRIMINALITY ISSUE

Criminality and high imprisonment rates of Mexican Americans are long-standing issues that have to be approached with the intentions of resolving the many factors that play a role in their causation. There are no easy or quick solutions for the problem; each of the causal factors involved requires understanding, perseverance, and innovative approaches for resolution. It is a fact that Mexican Americans and African Americans, are more likely to be arrested and sentenced to jail for equivalent crimes including drug-related crimes, than non-Hispanic whites. This is an outcome of racial profiling and the lower socioeconomic status of the offenders who therefore cannot cover the cost of adequate legal defense.

Criminality begins with the environment in which many Mexican American and Hispanic American children are raised, where there are high rates of criminality including drug dealing and use, and gang activity. It continues with school absenteeism and abandonment, poor parental control and biased police involvement. Once an individual is charged with a crime, there is generally an inadequate defense and a jail term is unavoidable. In jail, conditions worsen with pressure from other, more seasoned prisoners. When released from prison, there is hopelessness, lack of employment, and recidivism. In order to resolve the problem this fatal cycle must be interrupted.

In the short-term police involvement should be part of the solution. Law enforcement by police should be different from the usual approach in the treatment of minorities which is characterized by intolerance, roughness, and unyielding force, not infrequently, with use of brutality. The kind of police intervention needed for Mexican American youths is of the old-fashioned type, gentle but firm, paternal and as friendly as possible. Police should not expect most interventions to end with arrest, but should be prepared to give advice and expect compliance and respect for the law. Arrest of a young person can be, and not infrequently is, the beginning of a criminal career. Police training has to be modified. Sensitivity training to the needs of the Hispanic population must be part of the training. This applies equally to Hispanic and Anglo police because the present behavior of abuse, particularly towards the weak, the minority young, the poor, and the uneducated is similar with both groups. In many ways the present behavior of police towards minorities is frequently not different from that which exist in countries governed by despots. Frequently, police intervention in youthful misbehavior is a recipe for adult criminality.

Police-family interaction similar to parent-teacher associations could be extremely helpful and should start early in pre-school years and continue through high school. At these police-family meetings it should be stressed that civil behavior and observance of the law, are values that should be taught at home. The police role should be primarily that of support for the parents, and their behavior should be friendly rather than authoritarian. Police patrolling to be more effective in Mexican American neighborhoods should be as much as possible on foot. Preferably the patrol should be carried out by Mexican American, or other Hispanic or non-Hispanic whites who have been re-trained in law enforcement for minorities. A return to the era of the corner cop, known and respected, not feared by the neighborhood is what is needed.

To solve the problems of the imprisoned population, which in the United States is greater than in any other democratic country, a new approach must be tried. As is well known, the prison population in this country is mostly Hispanic and African American. The initial reason for prison is frequently drug related. In jail, behavior is racist and violent without any meaningful preparation for life after release. Release from prison is more frequently than not, followed by recidivism and the beginning of a lifelong crime career.

African American and Hispanic leaders must get together and devise programs to keep young men and women out of prison and programs designed to avoid recurrence of criminal activity.

Given the nature of American democracy, it will be difficult to gain acceptance from the public and from the government to put in practice what would probably be the best solution. What is being proposed, Americans criticize the Chinese for doing—that is putting prisoners to work. There are many reasons why released prisoners return to a life of crime but some of the most significant are lack of skills and unemployment because of their criminal record. If prisoners could be trained in a real job by civilian employers who would benefit from their developed skills and be recognized by them as valuable employees, they may be accepted after release from prison into employments in the community. This would allow for easier, more rational treatment and more likely lead to successful re-integration into society.

This could be the way the proposed system would work. Industry and other employers could be invited and give incentives to establish places of work within or in the vicinity of the jail facility. If possible, jails could be built or re-located near work sources. Prisoners would be provided with low wages while in training and while in prison. The same employer would have places of work within the community and the prisoners would be given employment there, after release. At that point the released prisoner, now a member of the community, would be given living wages.

Other possible solutions to the problem of criminality exists, but any solution should provide recognition of the factors that cause it. Jail in itself is not redeeming unless good reasons and means are provided to avoid return to a criminal life. Meaningful work training is one. That is the challenge that America as a whole faces, and it requires, we need a solution even if the solution is difficult and seemingly impossible or initially unacceptable.

Mexican American and all Hispanics must play a more vital role in this country. Time is short and is being wasted as we speak. There is much work to be done. The road is not easy, but we must begin to travel it, with unity and faith in the ultimate good results. The United States and all of us will be better for the effort.

There are many good things happening in Mexican American education. A great deal still remains to be done but there are great reasons for hope. As Mexican Americans we have to remember that our presence in this country began most humbly. First treated as the loser in the Texas independence and accused of being anti-Texan and anti-American. Then the loss of the Mexico-United States war reduced Mexican Americans to second-class citizenship. Then the multiple revolutions that happened in Mexico forced many of our people to become refugees. Many of those who came to the country at that time were low-skilled individuals who augmented the low-skilled labor supply. Later yet came the wave of Mexicans in the Bracero program. After that program ended, Mexican Americans became frequently the undocumented workers who still worked in horrible conditions as migrant workers.

In contrast, other Hispanics have migrated as professionals and often with certain economic means. Puerto Ricans are American citizens and migrate at will to the United States. Cubans came as a privileged, politically protected class and were at least at the time of their arrival the landowners and the professional and business class in Cuba. They left Cuba escaping from the Castro revolution. In Cuba they left behind the peasants from whom the Cuban government has to depend now. Cuban Americans have contributed significantly to Florida, rescued Miami from slums, made Miami rich and a fun place to visit. Central Americans share many of the problems that Mexican Americans have. The present Central American migrants are getting help mostly from the Mexican Americans population and from local churches who do it in a show of friendship and compassion. Dangers to immigrants are too high in the Mexican side of the border. Trump and his policies make refugees stay in Mexico while allowing exceedingly few to reach a court of law to plead their case. Those courts frequently delay or refuse to grant refugee status.

Asians including Indians, Chinese, and Koreans have the distinct advantage of having arrived with a profession, usually as doctors of medicine or engineers and having been welcomed with green cards and employment in lucrative positions.

So, yes, our Mexican American people have much to lament from our humble beginnings and more of a century of ill-treatment by European Americans especially Texan European Americans, so-called Anglos, but also by non-Hispanic Arizonians and Californians They were horrible in the treatment of Mexicans and Mexican Americans often with the consent of state and federal governments. But let us not fault them for behavior that unfortunately is ours. For too long we have acted as the victims. Now we have to work harder to solve our problems. Yes, we have to work harder but mostly do our duty. It is very much up to us.

Let us be proud American citizens. Let us vote in all elections, embrace education, fight for our rights, and help protect the undocumented. Work tirelessly in challenging occupations. Favor our own and other Hispanics. Fight against those who insult and discriminate against us, Take care of our family and our health. Lastly forget the lies and fantasies surrounding the Alamo battle. Mexicans were not cruel; the Mexican soldiers were doing their duty and many died in the battle. There was only one cruel Mexican, General Santa Ana who actually with his actions in Texas and throughout Mexico victimized vastly many more Mexicans by far, than those of the Alamo and Goliad defenders.

MEXICAN AMERICAN PRIDE
PRINCIPLE NUMBER 3

I will educate myself so I become an informed person.

 ISSUES TO BE DISCUSSED UNDER THIS PRINCIPLE:

1. Knowledge is important for all individuals but is particularly important for Mexican Americans.

2. The quest for knowledge is lifelong but begins within the family confines.

3. The lessons of history are important for all Americans and should be heeded to avoid future disastrous events.

4. Mexican Americans, legal immigrants, and American citizens, were deported to Mexico during the depression years. This event may be repeated, and sooner rather than later.

5. Mexican Americans need strong leaders willing to challenge unjust laws and discrimination.

6. Mexican American and Hispanics are easy victims of discriminatory practices and abuse.

7. Mexican American and Hispanics need to be ready to maintain American leadership in the world.

Knowledge is an indispensable tool in every individual's life. Knowledge is acquired in multiple ways. The first education begins at home through the influence of our parents, close relatives and extended family. This early education influences our behavior towards school and other institutions, towards society, towards our nation and the world. In some very definite ways this first educational experience often shapes and greatly influences the rest of our lives.

School is the next step in our learning process, and it helps prepare us for the future. What we learn in school widens our horizon and permits us to define what our particular role in society will be. School can have the greatest influence in helping to identify our future occupation. Success in academic learning is one of the keys to a successful life for an individual and for his or her family. To succeed in this country, the minimum educational level needed is high school. This attainment is needed to be able to transition to college education. Lack of high school graduation, generally guarantees a life of hardship. Now that technology, engineering, and medicine may be the most important job-generating areas, college education is particularly necessary.

In a definitive way the lower rate of high school graduation of Mexican Americans is the reason for the low socioeconomic status of the group. Every Mexican American and every Hispanic should make education the priority that other national groups in the country give it. Every Mexican American and Hispanic should work to complete their high school education if for some reason they did not do it at the normal age. The younger the individual is, the better opportunity to go back to high school. If going back to school is not an option, by all means work to obtain a GED certificate (equivalent of high school certification for some purposes). This certification may help to avoid some hardships caused by lack of a high school diploma.

Education does not end with completion of school learning whatever its level, even if this level is professional. Educational influences and opportunities are all around and are both positive and negative in character. The influence of radio, television, and movies is ever-present and is for the most part negative, designed to entertain rather than to inform or educate.

The information is often biased, designed to support individual agendas and political views. It is often alarmist and misleading. Good judgment is needed on the part of the individual to fully interpret the validity and reliability of the news these media provide.

The internet is a great source of information. No subject is impossible to find on the internet. Just as with other media, the information obtained on the internet needs to be considered carefully. In fact, information on the internet requires more critical evaluation since it is at times published by sources and authors having a selfish, even negative or destructive agenda. Cell phones and their easy access to the internet and social media are addictive for all ages but especially for the young.

The foregoing condemnation of news sources does not mean that there are no good sources of information. We all can profit from various news and information sources including: Public Radio and Public Television, Discovery Channel, National Geographic, History, Animal Planet, Smithsonian Channel, Univision. Online there are many educational resources starting with WIKIPEDIA and the Pew research Center.

The judgment necessary to interpret the world around us and the significance of events of importance is only acquired through reading a number of sources that can expand our knowledge. For Mexican Americans it is of the utmost importance to read about American and Mexican history and geography and about the race relations brought about by the Mexican-American war and its aftermath. Readings should include the influence of the Mexican revolution on immigration to the United States, and the forced return of Mexican and Mexican Americans during the Depression of the late 1920s and early 1930s, even though many of them were legal immigrants or American citizens. It is particularly important to be aware of the past treatment of Mexican Americans, to realize the importance and the history behind the present anti-immigrant feelings directed not only against illegal immigration, but also against Mexicans, Mexican Americans, and Hispanics.

The fear generated by racist, radical, popularity, and ratings-seeking individuals, such as those journalists and editors at Fox Network, could only be the beginning of a more general anti-Hispanic attitude that all Hispanics should unite to prevent. Realize that although it is estimated that in 2017 there were somewhere between 10.5 and 11 million undocumented immigrants of all continents, nationalities, and races, the anti-immigrant fear and rhetoric is predominantly directed towards the Mexican undocumented who number perhaps less than five million. The number of undocumented Mexican immigrants is decreasing and is a negative flow—more Mexicans going back to Mexico than coming to the United States.

In the process of identifying and targeting illegal aliens, damage is done to all Hispanics who become victims of racial profiling. The situation is made much worse by President Trump who is stoking fear among the white population and relying on white supremacists for re-election support. Therefore, the issue of illegal immigration is extremely important to all Hispanic Americans. There is no mention of the undocumented of European or Asian origin, particularly if a person is of European stock. In any programs to reduce illegal immigration the battle is directed almost exclusively against Hispanics, Mexican Americans, and Mexicans.

It is extremely important for Mexican Americans and Hispanics to understand the fear among non-Hispanic whites that their world is changing. The "Make America Great Again" battle cry of Trump is actually an attempt to make America white again. He and the entire white population know that this is impossible and that they must adapt to the present and coming reality. We must reassure them that the greatness of the United States will be preserved by us. That is a great responsibility that we must be prepared to take.

Everyone should be aware of the dictum that all those who do not remember (or do not know) history are condemned to live it again. For Mexican Americans history is particularly cruel and must not be allowed to be repeated. The various anti-immigrant, anti-Mexican, and anti-Hispanic events of late could be the beginning of another wave of negative, highly discriminatory practices spurred by hateful individuals and racist hate groups. Hispanics must not allow this to happen. The answer to these actions is unity and strength. Hispanic leaders must rise to the occasion the way black leaders have, but the responsibility is for all of us to own.

The freedom that blacks enjoy today, still far from what is socially just, is due to the sacrifice of early leaders and the vigilance of those of the present. The media is afraid of black leaders such as Reverend Jackson or Reverend Al Sharpton. Hispanics however seem to be fair game to the likes of most Fox News broadcasters and most members of the Trump cabinet. We could use Hispanic leaders like the African Americans have; we could use even radical leaders such as Malcolm X. Mexican Americans and Hispanics, including our leaders, are much too compliant, tame, cautious, and pacifist, willing to give up without a fight or even without protest.

We might have to change our natural tendencies to be conformist, fatalistic, and demand more respect for our ancestry. As Americans of Hispanic descent, we must be prepared to improve ourselves in every way needed to reach equality with the most respected groups, but we also must be ready to defend those of us who are so unfairly attacked and discriminated against.

Necessary readings for all, also includes European and world history and geography, the rise to power and fall of states and nations over the centuries, religious influences that shaped the arts, sciences, and the conflicts generated by religious differences. Racial and religious conflicts have shaped history over the centuries, continue to do so today, and we should be aware of them. We should be aware of international news, dealing with international relations, commercial relations, conflicts and rivalries, particularly those affecting the United States. Environmental changes including global warming, impact on nature, effects of overpopulation, man's impact on animal life, ocean pollution, and forest depletion are subjects that everyone should become familiar with, offer and act responsibly with some personal solutions. The environment is so critically important. Do something.

General knowledge and awareness are necessary for understanding present and future situations; it also stimulates creativity and enterprise. American Ingenuity, enterprise and creativity in turn, represents perhaps the greatest contribution from America to the world. Every American needs to participate in these activities to maintain America's leading position in the world. Hispanics will be the most numerous Americans in the future and all of us must be prepared to make the necessary contributions to keep the United States in that leading position. Better prepared Mexican Americans and Hispanic Americans are essential to maintain not only the leading position of the United States but perhaps to make an America that is more compassionate and understanding of people who are different, more in tune and cooperative with the rest of the world. Perhaps at that time, the idea that the United States must be the world policeman will stop. It would be much better for this country and for the world, if instead of being the world policeman, we joined in a world police force that would include the European Union, Canada, Australia, Brazil, Russia, and perhaps China, Japan, India as well as other willing countries.

MEXICAN AMERICAN PRIDE
PRINCIPLE NUMBER 4

I will learn to read, speak, and communicate
in English in addition to Spanish.

THE POINTS UNDER DISCUSSION UNDER THIS PRINCIPLE INCLUDE THE FOLLOWING:

1. Mexican Americans have strong attachment to the Spanish language. This is a barrier to English proficiency, particularly in areas of high Mexican American population.

2. Misunderstandings between Mexicans and Mexican Americans are common and frequently related to use of Spanish language

3. Other sources of misunderstandings are the differences between educational systems in the two countries, the perception of graft corruption in Mexico, and the rise of criminal activity in the border areas and across Mexico.

4. The need for English speaking varies across Mexican American groups and the condition known as ethnic dilution.

5. English proficiency is the essential key for the progress of Mexican Americans in this country.

6. The first and greatest responsibility for English proficiency in

children rests at home, with their parents. Parents must provide an environment conducive to learning and using English.

7. Schools can help promote English proficiency greatly by using methods that encourage English use.

8. All mechanisms that encourage use of English by Mexican Americans should be employed. This includes communities and the businesses that serve them.

9. Scholastic performance testing may require some fine-tuning to avoid a bias toward English speakers. This fine-tuning should not impair testing objectivity.

10. English proficiency is of primary importance for Mexican Americans, but Spanish-speaking ability is also important.

Mexican Americans have strong attachment to Spanish. This is particularly true for recent Mexican immigrants and for first generation born in this country. Along with the language they also are strongly attached to the music, celebrations, and costumes of Mexico. This is only natural because of the proximity to Mexico and because many of their relatives prefer to speak, or only speak Spanish.

The strong attachment to Spanish is particularly the case in areas of high Mexican American population and in the border areas. Here, it becomes very difficult for the average Mexican American to communicate in English, especially early in the process of learning the language. This is because if he or she attempts to communicate in English, the other person almost invariably answers in Spanish. In these areas of high Spanish-speaking concentration, people with better command of both languages, commonly mix both languages in conversation. This is the true Spanglish and people able to do it find it very natural and a very comfortable way to communicate.

Other barriers for Mexican Americans to perfect or master their English in the border areas is the commercial ties to Mexican customers, since these customers expect people looking like them to speak Spanish. Mexicans do not seem to realize that some Mexican Americans do not speak Spanish out of haughtiness but because they do not speak it at all or do not speak it well enough. After all this is an English-speaking country where English fluency is essential to succeed.

There is another group for whom English is essential. In fact, this group of Mexican Americans and Hispanics may not identify themselves as Hispanic or Latin and may never have learned and are certainly not fluent in Spanish. These are the products of intermarriage between Mexican American and non-Hispanic whites, or other races. This group also includes those Mexican Americans who, as a result of their upbringing or circumstances, may not ordinarily come in contact with Spanish speakers and may not even consider themselves Hispanic or Mexican American. These groups are now recognized as the result of a situation called ethnic dilution.

There is a great deal of misunderstanding between Mexicans and Mexican Americans not infrequently related to language. The Spanish spoken by many Mexican Americans may have an American accent or be somewhat archaic, and at times resembles the Spanish spoken in Mexico at the time of the Mexican-American war utilizing word forms no longer in use in Mexico. It resembles the situation of Quebec French versus the French spoken in France or the German still spoken in some areas in the United States. This type of Spanish is still spoken in isolated regions of Mexico; therefore, Mexicans equate use of this type of Spanish, wrongly, equivalent to lack of education. Mexican Americans at times adopt English words making them sound like Spanish but often not resembling true Spanish words. This misunderstanding causes great stress among the two groups and even among related families.

Educational systems in the United States and Mexico are different. This difference is also a source of misunderstanding between Mexicans and Mexican Americans. It is important for Mexicans to realize that Mexican Americans face different problems that those faced by Mexicans in their struggle to improve their lives. Education is much more expensive in the

United States and it generally takes longer to graduate for equivalent levels of education. Mexican physicians, engineers, and all other professionals graduate at a younger age. Most importantly they graduate without the heavy weight of a huge student debt. While most Mexicans have access to a free or nearly free education, for Mexican Americans it is an upward and frequently insurmountable barrier to college education.

Another source of irritation between Mexican Americans and Mexicans is the problem of graft and corruption, which until recently was everywhere in Mexico, particularly among police and border officials. The problem of corruption has improved, but the problem of crime related to drug trafficking and criminality in general, including kidnapping for ransom, is much worse than it used to be in Mexico. It is hoped that authorities can address crime reduction, but for the time being it is a very serious problem. While the problem of corruption was mostly annoying, criminality has become a true deterrent to travel into Mexico for Mexican Americans as it is for all Americans and even Mexicans. The problems created by the drug traffic are much worse for Mexicans than for Americans since in Mexico, innocent lives are at times caught in the crossfire between rival criminal gangs or between drug criminals and authorities. The fear of crime has created a new type of legal Mexican immigrant. These immigrants are for the most part wealthy Mexicans running away from Mexico because of the danger of kidnapping and other serious criminal activity.

If for recent immigrants English is not seen as a priority, for successive generations English becomes essential for progress on a personal and societal level. Studies that show that second generation Hispanic Americans are highly proficient in English. They feel they speak English very well in over 80% of cases and by third generation nearly 100% feel that way. English use, therefore, should not be a problem for Mexican Americans. In areas of high population of bilingual Mexican Americans, they still prefer to continue communicating in the language traditional for the family. This situation may never change given the strong family relationships across the border and in Mexican American areas, where extended families are common.

Bilingualism gives origin to the use of Spanglish in conversations between Mexican Americans and also between all Hispanic Americans. Spanglish might be a good way for adult English learners to become accustomed to using English. It would certainly be better for beginners to use Spanglish for communication rather than not using English at all, as it is frequently the case in the borderlands. It is not well known to what extent bilingualism affects performance in academic achievement testing, compared to performance by English speakers only. It is possible that this type of testing is somewhat biased in favor of English speakers only and needs to be modified to reflect true academic performance scores between the two groups. This, of course, is a complex issue that needs careful study and thoughtful resolution. Bilingual Spanish and English speakers should not need special testing methods but some fine-tuning may be necessary to avoid bias.

It is imperative for all Mexican American and Hispanic American parents in Spanish-speaking households to encourage their children to learn and use English. English use at home must be encouraged; it is the duty of responsible and caring parents to do so. One way parents can promote English use is by requiring children to watch educational and entertainment television programs in English instead of allowing them to watch Spanish television channels only. Schools should promote debating clubs and other programs to increase English proficiency and use of high-level English. Bilingual programs if used in early school years should be intense and designed to produce English proficiency as early as possible. Bilingual programs should only be necessary in the English learning process for recent older children émigrés not for children born in the United States. Spanish language television channels could help English learning and proficiency by providing simultaneous translations where possible. Proficiency in English is the essential key to progress for Mexican Americans and for all Hispanics; every effort should be made by all who can help, for this to happen. Involvement in this effort must include the entire community and the businesses that serve them. For example, employees should be required to answer in English when the customer addresses them in English.

To be able to communicate in both languages offers a distinct advantage as the Hispanic American population becomes more prevalent in this country. To be bilingual in English and Spanish will become highly desirable as commercial and other relations with Latin America increase in importance to the United States. Spanish language training for Americans should be recognized for its strategic importance in relations with Latin American countries. Emphasis on English language proficiency in no way means that Spanish language skills are not important.

There is absolutely no question that for success in this country English language speaking is essential. Spanish is the natural second language and it may become in the future when better and more productive relations with Latin America become necessary.

It is also necessary and highly desirable that relations between Mexicans and Mexican Americans improve. The government of Mexico and its consular services must get involved for this improvement to happen. Mexico and Mexicans must understand that Mexican Americans are Americans and treat them as such. If Mexican Americans want to try their Spanish in conversation with Mexicans, that is great, and they deserve recognition and encouragement for that. On the other hand, Mexican American officials at the border entrance points seem to behave rudely and with little respect for visiting Mexicans. It seems that frequently Anglo guards are more welcoming and courteous than their Mexican American counterparts. This Mexican American border guard behavior is not acceptable and only increases misunderstandings. These guards could benefit from sensitivity training and the proper authorities should take responsibility for this.

Along with others I think that Mexicans and Mexican Americans should behave more like Jewish Americans whose second country in their heart is Israel. Let us follow their example. Let us have the best relations among these two groups of people who are more than just basically the same. "One people two nations."

MEXICAN AMERICAN PRIDE
PRINCIPLE NUMBER 5

> If I am not now, I will become
> an American citizen as soon as possible.

 IN THIS CHAPTER THE FOLLOWING CONCEPTS ARE DISCUSSED:

1. American citizenship is extremely valuable. Fulfilling its rights and duties are of the outmost importance for Mexican Americans.

2. It is similarly important for legal Mexican immigrants to become American citizens as soon as eligible and instill in their children the importance of being American citizens.

3. Not claiming citizenship and neglecting citizenship rights and duties perpetuates the idea of Mexican Americans being aliens in their own country.

4. Mexican Americans have to change past behavior and become active American citizens.

5. The reluctance to become citizens make Mexican Americans easy to ignore as voters and allow detractors to defeat Mexican American favorite candidates.

6. The Mexican American voter apathy assures opponents of easy election victories.

7. Mexican Americans do not have to give up traditions and celebrations of their Mexican heritage to act, feel and actively participate in the affairs of this country as full and true Americans.

8. Mexican Americans American citizenship is needed now. This will allow voting for passage of legislation on issues of importance to the group.

There is no more valuable citizenship on the world now, than that of being a citizen of the United States of America. This citizenship carries both duties and rights. Mexican Americans already take on the duties for the most part. Mexican Americans work and pay taxes like every other American national group work. Like every other group and indeed more so, Mexican Americans participate in the defense of this country. A great number of Mexican Americans serve and have served with distinction and pride in the armed forces of the United States. It is time for Mexican Americans to take seriously one other duty, the duty and the right to vote.

Over the years it has been traditional for legal Mexican immigrants in this country to keep their Mexican citizenship. At times this is displayed as a badge of honor. This lack of responsibility hurts all Mexican Americans because it perpetuates the idea that there is a certain alien feeling to Mexican Americans. "Yes, they are Americans but not in the same sense as European Americans." "They are Mexicans living in the United States." And so on, go the rationalizations. The fact is that Mexican Americans by not participating in their legitimate right to American citizenship become aliens in their own country. In more than one way, it also hurts Mexico, making Mexico by extension seem of less importance as a partner in diplomatic and commercial relations.

This alien perception gives some hysterical people of the conservative right a reason to attack both legal and illegal people of Mexican origin and by extension all Hispanics. They talk about Reconquista and the Plan of San Diego as evidence that Mexico is trying to take back the territories, she lost in the Plan of Guadalupe Hidalgo that concluded the Mexican American War. Writings such as the Plan of San Diego and Reconquista talk were only expressions of the great frustration that Mexican Americans felt at not being accepted as equals in the United States, and being victims of discrimination and mistreatment.

For some Mexican immigrants, implicit in the idea of keeping their Mexican citizenship is that one day, they will go back to Mexico. The years go by; they have children in this country, they stay in the United States, and they forget or they become too morose to apply for American citizenship. Worse than that, they neglect to instill the citizenship rights and duties in their children, who are often American citizens by birth. As a consequence of not having American citizenship, a large pool of potential voters gives up their power at the voting booth. Their ability to affect the course of the nation is therefore impaired. Mexicans and Mexican Americans become a pool of people who can be ignored, discarded, and thrown out of the country as recessions or other calamities affect the economy of the United States.

It is time to change; every legal Mexican immigrant must apply for American citizenship if they have not done so. It is time to stop being an alien. It hurts all Mexican Americans and deprives the nation of the needed participation of all its citizens in the affairs of the country. It is time to become Americans in thought and action.

All Mexican Americans all Hispanics and the entire nation will be better off if they all become American Citizens and voters. DREAMERS and their parents would get the support they need. Undocumented immigrants, would then have a reason to hope that someday they will stop suffering and feel free of fear. Fear for themselves and their families. For years they have hoped for the passage of new immigration legislation. For years they have been promised the legislation will be passed; they have been used as a political football mainly by the political parties. At times only a few votes are needed to pass the legislation, but the votes are not there. The needed votes could perhaps have been obtained if Mexican Americans would have voted for the right legislators. The needed right legislators were afraid to lose their seat, since the opposition, Republican voters always vote. And, Mexican Americans, famously, don't vote. Republicans know it. Everyone knows it. Texas knows it, Senator Cruz knows it. He won his senate seat back by less than 20,000 votes to defeat Beto O'Rourke when the votes of only some of the millions of Mexican Americans could have prevented Cruz from winning, but the votes were not there. Senator Cruz is Canadian born (not Canada's fault) from a Cuban father and an American mother. He has distinguished himself as being a rabid anti-immigrant and anti-Mexican American. He was elected by default by Mexican Americans who were either too lazy to go to the polls, or too uncaring to be good American citizens. Senator Cruz is an extremely smart individual but a horrible human being. He is happy to see Mexican Americans suffer. His background is Cuban, but he is happy to see the poor left in Cuba, suffer and die.

Recently Mexican Americans missed the opportunity of supporting a worthy Mexican American presidential candidate. Julian Castro could not gather enough support in a crowded candidate field. Castro is young, and we hope he enters the next presidential race. Mexican Americans have to have faith that one of their own can be president of the United States. Mexican Americans have to make sure he qualifies, then, as the leading candidate from the Democratic party.

To become American citizens, Mexican Americans, do not have to give up the traditions and celebrations of the Mexican spirit; these are for the most part noble and colorful contributions to the American culture. They are part of the diverse American tapestry including: English Americans, Irish Americans, Italian Americans, German Americans, and nearly every other national group. In this country all who share that ancestry find a way to celebrate their ancestral country traditions. That Mexican Americans do the same, should not be seen as a threat to the integrity and sovereignty of the United States.

The time to act to become an American citizen and to exercise the privilege of voting is now. In reality it was yesterday. Much damage has been done to Mexican Americans by their failure to not claim, defend, and exert their citizenship rights. If you, as a reader of this segment, are a legal Mexican immigrant who has not partaken of American citizenship rights and duties, you should start the process now. If you know someone who is in the same situation, make it your duty to talk to him or her. Believe me, the entire American nation will be better off because of the action you take.

Mexicans are still targeted for discrimination in this country, and President Trump considers Mexican and Mexican Americans thieves, rapists, invaders, and generally undesirable. Those opinions are shared by nativists and white supremacists along with people in the right-wing media such as Fox News. These thoughts are expressed without consequences, because Mexican Americans do not care to become citizens, and when citizens they do not vote. There are some Mexican Americans who did vote for Trump in spite of all the insults. Among the reasons they voted for Trump is because they are well to do and want to protect their wealth. They like the idea of paying lower taxes and are against programs to help the poor.

If we want to have a chance at a new immigration policy, where DREAMERS are accepted and undocumented immigrants have a chance at regularization, we have to vote. In this case we need to vote Democrat so that we have a better chance of improving our people. Democrats had a chance to do something for us when Obama was president, but he and his party opted to support other causes and only used us to get elected. In fact, the faith we placed in Obama turned out to be misguided. Let us make sure that doesn't happen again. We as Mexican Americans have to use our voting power wisely. If all of us vote, we can determine who governs us.

MEXICAN AMERICAN PRIDE
PRINCIPLE NUMBER 6

As an American citizen,
I will always exercise my voting rights.

 This section includes discussion of the following concepts:

1. The democratic form of government is the best and fairest of all the forms of government, but citizens need to understand the way it functions and need to fully participate to make democracy live UP to its potential.

2. There are problems in the way the American democracy functions including the issue of the inequality of its citizens.

3. A two-party political system is problematic for finding consensus on what is best for the nation and its citizens. A third party or a caucus of concerned legislators regardless of party affiliation would improve the function of the government.

4. The political needs of Mexican Americans are more closely in line with the policies of the Democratic Party. Historically neither the Democratic nor the Republican Party has been particularly helpful to Mexican Americans. Mexican Americans and Hispanics must be knowledgeable about the issues and vote for the best response to those issues and the best candidate

rather than along party affiliations. This fact should not prevent Mexican Americans from participating fully in the political process.

5. One of the greatest problems in our American democracy is the graft and corruption into which our elected officials are forced, when they take handouts from interest groups to get elected and re-elected. There is really no other name for the monetary and in-kind contributions from interest groups than graft. Publicly supported elections and spending limits are urgently needed. There is need for a permanent third political party.

6. The Supreme Court of the United States is supposed to be an apolitical body, but at times it makes partisan, detrimental decisions against the public good. Ideally members of the Supreme Court should be chosen for their fairness, their vision for the public good, and for the best interest of the citizens and the nation rather than for partisan political views.

7. Gerrymandering, the most frequently used mechanism for redistricting is an unfair mechanism used to perpetuate the party in power. Unfortunately, the Supreme Court has failed to rule its practice as unconstitutional and has in fact made it worse by allowing redistricting any time, instead of being tied to census results.

8. Citizens need to be aware of the biases and power of the press. In particular, the impact of radio and television, particularly television and radio commentators is highly concerning. They tend to distort facts according to their particular agendas, without regard for the truth. Citizens need to consult a number of sources to have a better, more informed opinion about issues crucial to the nation and its citizens.

9. For Mexican Americans steady participation in the political
    process is essential and will help to make real the promised
    "More perfect union" of the United States of America.

The most important right that an American citizen has, is the ability to choose the people who govern. By the same token, voting rights allow citizens to vote out those who do not do a good job of governing by electing someone else.

Most citizens agree some actions or work are important for the common good and expect their government to do them. Most issues of public concern are important to some people but not important or even detrimental to others. The way these issues are resolved is by electing people who will be wise and sensitive enough to find the best answer to the issue at hand. In a democracy such as ours, the majority in any issue is supposed to rule. However, there is a system of checks and balances at work so the rights of the minority are protected. In this way, the wishes and hopes of the minority on any issue are also taken into account.

As a short summary, the checks and balances of our democracy are found in the interplay of the three branches of government. The first is the legislative branch that enacts laws, including ordinances and rules of behavior. The second branch is the executive that executes or puts in practice the effects of the law. The third branch is the judicial branch that rules over the validity and the constitutionality of a rule, law or ordinance and is charged with the trial of all cases that involve the government. These three branches of government are found over the entire system, from the federal through the state and local level. In general, the federal laws rule over the state's laws and the states laws over the municipal or local laws.

The democratic principles of government have generally worked well for the country. The democratic form of government was initially formulated in antiquity by the Greeks and then practiced by the Romans. After the fall of Rome, democratic forms of government can scarcely be found until perfected by the United States in its quest for independence from England. Earlier forms of democratic governance were attempted and put into practice including the eventual enactment of the Magna Carta in English government in 1297. The Magna Carta limited the power of the King. Establishment of the democratic form of government in the United States inspired the French revolution and the declaration of human rights. Most of the countries in Latin America established democratic forms of government patterned after that of the United States after their independence from Spain, Portugal, and other European countries. Later, democratic forms of government were adopted in Europe and eventually in a large part of the world. While the democratic form of government has been maintained in the United States from the beginning, in other countries there have often been interruptions brought about by revolutions, armed or peaceful takeovers, transient dictatorships and attempts at other forms of government including communism.

The democratic form of government is without a doubt the best and fairest of all forms of government but is not by any means perfect, often requiring adjustments. Some of the adjustments are good and progressive, other adjustments are unwise, unfair, and detrimental.

Some of the problems:

The highest principle in our government, expressed in the Declaration of Independence of the United States, "All men are created equal" did not include blacks, women, Hispanics, or members of any race except white American males of European, Anglo-Saxon descent. Some progress has been attained over the years, but struggles by women, by African Americans, and particularly by Hispanics continue. Hispanics can best obtain justice and attain equality by exercising their citizen rights, prominently by voting at any level and about all issues. Unfair laws, ordinances and rules can be voted down. If adopted, they can be challenged by appealing to the courts. Other means available are through demonstrations, protest, and peaceful civilian disobedience as well as organized attempts to change the laws.

Hispanic leaders willing to make sacrifices as black leaders did and do, in attempting to change and right wrongs are greatly needed by Hispanics. Articulate, vociferous, and energetic leaders capable of inspiring the Hispanic people are essential to change the American unfair, dismissive, and discriminatory attitude towards the majority of Hispanic people, particularly the poor, the uneducated and the needy. The American dream is within reach for Hispanics but work is needed to attain it. Hispanic leaders as they appear on radio, television, and public appearances tend to be submissive, apologetic, and poor orators. Gain cannot be obtained without struggle and pain. Hispanics, particularly Mexican Americans have to become better educated, more active, more accepting of challenge, and more willing to challenge the system. The indolence, conformism, and fatalism that characterizes the Mexican American overall behavior has to be replaced with energy, hard work, and optimism. The "Si Dios quiere" and "Que sea por Dios" attitude must be replaced with "let's do it" and "No, you won't do that to us."

A second and great problem in this country is the two-party political system in government. On one side is the Democratic Party which is the party of liberal thinking, its membership is diverse and includes most of the minorities, labor unions and socially conscious individuals. On the other side, the Republican Party is the conservative party and is generally inclusive of the rich, well to do, capitalistic, white individuals with token representation from minorities. Although both parties include wealthy individuals, the Democratic Party is more socially responsive and the Republican Party is more representative of the ruling class. The two-party system is a problem because more often than not, the middle of the road on any issue is not well represented. So-called bipartisan work and behavior is practically nonexistent now, and compromise on the issues is rarely attained, meaning the best possible outcome for the nation is lost. A third party even if much smaller in power, could function as the give and take that is needed as an equalizer, as a security valve to reach the best consensus.

Third parties have frequently emerged in the election panorama. Third party candidates occur mainly around the time of presidential elections. Some of these parties remain in a state of hibernation emerging from time to time. The Libertarian party, The Green party are the most predominant. The Tea party is lurking in the guts of the Republican party and includes the more radical, anti-immigrant, anti-Hispanic white supremacist wing of the Republican party. All of the previously mentioned third parties are not the kind of third party the nation needs. The third party the nation and Hispanics need is a permanent third party. Just as permanent as the Republican or Democratic party. It does not have to be a big party. It has to be small enough that honest consensus within the members can exist. It has to be a party that only considers and supports what is best for the governed. It has to be a party that is free of the corrupting influence of interest groups. Most important it has to be a political party in which all members promise to vote in every election. It is possible that such a party may commence as a wing of the Democratic Party just as the Tea party arose from the Republic party.

Historically neither the Democratic nor the Republican Party has been particularly helpful to Mexican Americans. The Republican Party has been notoriously anti-Hispanic of late, being held captive by the extreme right that is basically opposed to affording equality to Mexican Americans and other Hispanics. They are the descendants and successors of the Anglos of older days, whose precepts were the inferiority of the Hispanic race and the rights of Anglos to take advantage of their real and perceived weaknesses. Both parties court the Hispanics with promises of re-dress their complaints and more attention to their needs. Mexican Americans are more likely to be courted by Democrats who offer solution to their various problems including more and better attention to the Mexican American veterans and solution of the undocumented immigrant situation. The Republican Party is more likely to court Cuban Americans with their eternal promise to get rid of Fidel and now that he is dead of Raul Castro and their communist government. Once in power, little is done to solve the Hispanic problems, since consensus requires compromise and compromise is a hard-bargaining piece. The solution to the Cuban dream of getting rid of Castro would require armed intervention, since nothing else has worked. This is hardly what the American public would agree to do. Meanwhile the only thing accomplished is more suffering imposed on the Cuban people who either cannot or will not abandon their country.

An extremely serious problem is the dependency of elected individuals upon interest groups. Elected individuals have to depend for their election and re-election of donations or contributions from interest groups, whose motive for giving economic support are the enactment of favorable laws and rules favorable to their particular interests. Often the result of this lobbying is unfavorable to the public at large. Not infrequently, these interest groups lend their expertise in the formulation of the laws and at times they themselves write the proposed law in its entirety, for consideration and enactment by the elected individual or individuals. Unfortunately, the Supreme Court of the nation has sanctioned the function of the lobbyists as legal and equates money given as the functional equivalent of citizen's votes. It is the dollar equals votes ruling, plus the ability of large interest groups to sway public opinion through propaganda, that keeps on harming the people of this nation and enriching the diverse industries that in such way thus dupe the public. The insurance industry, the pharmaceutical industry, the oil industry and the military-industrial complex of which Eisenhower warned us about, are frequent users of these tactics. Public support for elections and true limits on political spending are necessary to end these harmful practices but change is unlikely to happen given the power of interest groups to sway the system at will.

Eisenhower warned us about the fearsome power of the military-industrial complex. He was not around to know the present Medical-hospital-pharmaceutical-medical insurance complex. The power of these two organizational complexes is harming America and Americans. The first feeds American hubris; the second supposedly supports the free to choose medical system, while making medical care of Americans the most expensive and inefficient medical delivery system of any modern nation.

A significant problem is the makeup of the Supreme Court of the United States. Basically, Supreme Court members are nominated not for their fairness or their wise ways but for their political leanings, Democrat and liberal or Republican and conservative with proven track records of their political orientation. Changing rules for their confirmation by the Senate to simple majority instead of two thirds of its members is a frequent maneuver that should never be allowed. The simple majority rule also called the nuclear maneuver allows that a wise, fair and equity minded individual, who is also politically independent is never appointed to the Supreme Court. It should and must be an inviolable rule that a nominee to the Supreme Court needs two thirds of the Senate give its approval for confirmation. If necessary, a constitutional amendment must be sought. Somewhat to their credit, Supreme Court members issue rulings that most, but certainly not all of the times appear to be just, reaching a measure of fairness.

Gerrymandering is a redistricting strategy used by political parties to perpetuate their power and dilute the power of the opposite party. Gerrymandering has been used to deny legitimate groups including Hispanics the ability to win elections. The strategy calls for changing district boundaries in order to pack a district with opposition voters where the opposition was sure to win anyway, or diluting the opposition voters in districts where the margin to win is close thus favoring the party in power and most frequently the use of both tactics. This tactic is obviously anti-democratic by a fair observer, but the Supreme Court has been unable to make a decision about its unconstitutionality. Redistricting should be tied to the census in response to changes in population and should be ideally performed by a fair method that avoids gerrymandering. Many such methods exist and are used now in Canada, England, and some European nations.

There are mathematical methods of district re-drawing that could obviate the bias of gerrymandering and a few states are beginning to use these methods. The recent case of gerrymandering in Texas ostensibly to increase the power of Republicans in the state was overall declared constitutional by the Supreme Court of the United States. That was an unfortunate decision that not only legalized that particular redistricting but also allows redistricting at any time, without ties to the census. That Supreme Court decision stimulates the antidemocratic practice of gerrymandering, lengthening the day where a fair method of redistricting is practiced in the United States.

Not to be dismissed is the power of the press that can sway popular opinion in a major way. Television has the ability to enhance and destroy personalities, induce the entire country to a state of hysteria and distort all facts. The same can be said of radio commentators. They both helped the country to go to war in Iraq by presenting distorted views on the issue of weapons of mass destruction, by giving a negative impression of the United Nations inspectors as well as by stirring a negative impression of the opinion of other countries, most of which were and still are, our allies. As a consequence of these biased presentations, the American public was overwhelmingly encouraged to support pursuing war rather than allowing time for United Nations inspectors to conclude their investigations. Television commentators often overwhelm guests with opposite views by shutting them out and by having the last word on the issue under discussion. One of the better ways to obtain news without bias is Public Radio and Public Television. It is hard to obtain accurate and fair news from the rest of the world. Some newspapers and magazines do a fair job of presenting international news and facts. Another fair source of international news is the British Broadcasting System (BBC). The best way to maintain ourselves informed is to read a number of printed sources.

The dismal voting record of Mexican Americans is without a doubt the most important deterrent to the fair treatment, the continuing discriminatory practices against them, and to their lack of recognition as real Americans. Mexican Americans continue to refuse to become citizens and refuse to exercise the citizens' rights. That lack of voting encourages detractors to further restrict Mexican Americans rights. Even from the moment of birth Mexican Americans are threatened with birth certificate delays and denials. With obstetric hospital care as expensive as it is, many women choose home delivery of their babies by midwives. Some states including Texas use the midwife delivery to label the birth as suspicious.

Some states also deny passports based on the same suspicions. Denials of passport validity at times occur to Mexican Americans upon returning to the United States leaving them stranded abroad and in fact turning them stateless. There are frequent attempts to deny birth right citizenship. Trump particularly uses that threat to intimidate his opponents. There is yet another new tactic being tried, that is the restriction of voting by not renewing or cancelling voting registration to those people who do not vote in a certain number of consecutive elections.

As can be concluded in spite of the predictions, the rising power of Mexican Americans because their rising numbers may not happen. This is because the people who can vote refuse to do so. In fact, threats to disfranchise the Mexican American voter are strong and likely to win if the Mexican Americans voting behavior does not change.

It is important, then, for Mexican Americans to vote in all elections. Primaries as well as national, state, and local elections are all important. Perhaps one day in the future, Mexican American and Hispanics can be unified in their opinion and vote as such. That day will bring real power to Hispanics to counterbalance the power of detractors. When enough Hispanics, African Americans, and other minorities are elected, a Minority political party may not be necessary to have a good representation of minority rights. A minority caucus can then be organized in the Congress and Senate that could function somewhat independently. Women, Mexican Americans, Hispanics and other minorities must work for a day when we have a "More perfect Union" as the preamble to the Constitution of the United States promises.

MEXICAN AMERICAN PRIDE
PRINCIPLE NUMBER 7

> I will participate in political affairs
> as a voter and if possible as a candidate.

1. The ability to vote is an important and powerful right of citizens but is only a part of the political process in which Mexican Americans need more involvement.

2. Mexican immigrants all too often neglect acquiring American citizenship causing harm to Mexican American causes for generations. Every effort should be made to remedy this situation.

3. Citizens need to get acquainted with the issues and the agenda of candidates for office prior to voting. Particular attention should be paid for compatibility with issues of importance to Mexican Americans.

4. When listening to television or radio programs citizens have to realize that much of the information provided is biased and partisan, in line with the political orientation of the broadcaster and the stations owners.

5. Mexican Americans should be careful in choosing political party allegiance. The Democratic Party seems to be more in

line with the political needs of Mexican Americans; however, over time neither party has been particularly helpful to Mexican American causes. It is more important to be well informed about candidates and issues. In time, consideration should be given to formation of a minority political party or at least an effective caucus of minorities in Congress.

6. It is extremely important to increase voter registration of Mexican Americans. Great potential for Mexican Americans political ability and power is being lost due to lack of participation.

7. Mexican Americans should be more involved in party politics working for election of particular candidates who appear more aware of and sympathetic towards Mexican American causes.

8. Mexican Americans can and should elect more Mexican Americans to higher positions in state and federal governments. More Mexican Americans can and should participate as candidates.

9. Look in the ballots for Mexican American and Hispanic candidates to support.

10. Do the ultimate duty of an American citizen: study the issues and offer yourself as a candidate.

Exercising the right and duty to vote is one of the most important acts entrusted to and vested in an American citizen. Mexican Americans are among the lowest participants in this regard and this situation must change. Participating in the political process of the nation means more than voting. It means getting involved at many levels.

The first level of involvement is becoming a United States citizen. Many Mexican immigrants do not bother to become citizens of this country out of indifference. Other Mexican immigrants neglect becoming citizens because of a certain allegiance to Mexico and because they hold the belief that one day they will go back. Mexican Americans have the lowest rate of naturalization than any other national group. Many if not most of these immigrants bring up their families in the United States or have their children in this country. Because these individuals and couples are not interested in the affairs of the country, a sense and spirit of neglect for the duties of American citizenship is perpetuated in that family environment. This is one of the most important reasons for the low status of Mexican Americans in this country. Mexican immigrants must take very seriously their need to become citizens of the United States. They should stop harming their own future and the future of their children and grandchildren, because their neglect will negatively affect many generations of Mexican Americans after them.

Because of the problem of Mexican immigrants neglecting to become American citizens, the first duty of their children is to educate their parents about the need to become American citizens. Just as important, these parents must take their American citizenship seriously and fully, as most European immigrants do. They must make the transition and feel, act, and behave as true and proud Americans in regards to their civic duties. Relatives, neighbors and friends of Mexican immigrants should participate in the process of their Americanization. Convincing Mexican immigrants of the need to naturalize, should be seen as showing concern for them, their families, all Mexican Americans, and for the nation.

The second step in political involvement is to become informed about the candidates for office; it is of the utmost importance to know their position about issues important to citizens and particularly issues critical to Mexican Americans. Every candidate for any office should be graded for their compatibility and sensitivity towards Mexican American and Hispanic issues. If a candidate for office, no matter how high or low has a negative racist or insensitive feeling towards Mexican Americans, such attitude must be brought to light and condemned. It is also important to be well informed about other issues that affect citizens, such as different propositions that are invariably presented at election cycles. Being well and accurately informed about the issues and particularly about candidates is a daunting process.

With the seven-day twenty-four-hour news services competing for ratings, the public gets bombarded with information. Most of this information is geared to a certain purpose that fits the particular political orientation of the broadcaster and the broadcasting station. Newscasters would like nothing better than being the main factor in the election of their favorite candidate. Newscasters do not like settled situations or facts because that does not sell news. Intrigue, distortion of the facts and figures, changes in projections and polls, looking for real or perceived negative campaigning and negative presentations of a candidate's views, is what brings them viewers and sells advertising.

Another important level of involvement is choosing allegiance to a political party or choosing to be an independent voter. In our democracy, for practical purposes there are only two political parties. Most other nations with a democratic system of government have a functional multiparty system. In the United States, a third party has occasionally been formed but without much success in having a candidate elected. At election time several parties obtain a few votes each. The Green Party, the Libertarian Party and Socialist Parties are some of the regulars. At times, third parties have functioned as spoilers for a party that has members with a similar orientation, but championing slightly different causes. Also, occasionally individuals running as independents have been successful in being elected. It would be interesting if a third party made of Hispanics and other minorities could be formed, but for the time being, realistically, there are only two political party choices either the Democratic Party or the Republican Party. Mexican Americans should be attentive to the issues more than to an individual party or individual candidate and vote accordingly. To vote a straight ballot should be considered carefully and most or all of the time avoided.

Voter registration is a major contribution to the democratic process. Registration of Mexican Americans is extremely important for the progress of the Mexican American population. Statistics show that Hispanics make up approximately 12% of the population of the United States but only 4% of the registered voters. There are also efforts directed towards the disfranchisement of minorities with the pretext of assuring that all voters are legitimate citizens. Registration drives are important efforts to assure that as many Mexican Americans as possible are registered to vote. It is equally important to fight efforts at disfranchising minorities.

The next level of involvement in the political process is to work for a party or for the election of a candidate. Direct appeal, telephonic appeal and helping in a number of ways are welcomed by candidates and parties. Driving voters to polling places and monetary contributions are other ways to be involved. Mexican Americans should donate to the candidate of their choice. Voter participation in elections is very poor in the United States resulting in a minuscule minority of eligible voters determining the winning candidates. If a sizable percentage of Mexican Americans and Hispanics would vote, they could be a real factor in determining who governs this country. Mexican Americans and all Hispanics should and must work to attain the highest possible turn out on election day.

Then, of course there is the highest level of involvement in the political process; being a candidate for office or for a position in any governing body. Mexican Americans must be prepared to offer themselves as candidates for office. In fact, many Mexican Americans do so, at local levels and some at state level. More involvement is needed at the highest levels of government in the United States. Mexican Americans need to elect more Senators, more members to the House of Representatives more Governors of states and of course, presidential or vice-presidential candidates.

There is a need to have Mexican Americans in line for cabinet positions and as candidates for the Supreme Court. It is noteworthy that Cuban Americans have managed to attain significant positions in government despite being relative newcomers. This should indicate to Mexican Americans that more involvement in the political process is needed and that success in this regard is highly attainable.

To elect Mexican Americans at higher levels of government we have to be unified in mind and in fact. The forces that keep Mexican Americans from attaining political power are always at work. Success begins with Mexican Americans themselves. Let's become well informed and proud

American citizens—unified, conscious of our duties and our strengths. Let's show pride in our Mexican American heritage. We can do it!

In every state and in every community with significant Mexican American population there are individuals who can be successful as candidates for local, state and federal government positions. These possible candidates should be identified, encouraged and supported with funds and volunteers to promote their campaigns and election. Volunteers are extremely important, for registering voters, gathering funds and by building up a network of possible supports and voters. The recent near defeat of Ted Cruz by Beto O'Rourke in Texas, shows us how it can be done. Although Beto is not Mexican American he showed us how a sympathetic individual like him can raise enthusiasm among Mexican Americans. In that election young Mexican Americans became enthusiastic supporters. They often went door to door talking and registering voters and turning them into supporters. It is encouraging that young Mexican Americans can become so involved in elections. It shows that Mexican Americans are ready to master their destiny. A very hopeful sign indeed.

It is encouraging and heartwarming that for the first time in recent times a Mexican American entered the Democratic Party contest for the presidency of the United States. He did not gather enough support to continue his candidacy this time. However, his campaign raised significant issues related to the poor, to minorities, and to immigrants. Let us hope that Julian Castro will consider running as a candidate at the next opportunity. He deserves the support of all Mexican Americans. Hopefully he would also be the choice of all our Hispanic brothers and sisters. We need to encourage him to persist in his quest. We hope that by then, many more Mexican Americans will be registered and ready to lend support to one of our own.

Throughout the country at every election me have the opportunity to support Mexican American and Hispanic individuals who offer their service to us as candidates for a number of elected positions. Look for their names and vote for them.

The ultimate act of citizenship is to offer yourself as candidate. Study the issues behind the proposed position. Gather as much information as you can and be prepared to support your proposal with the necessary background information. Finally throw your hat in the ring and ask for support from your friends and the public in general. Support of volunteers to spread the word and economic support for your candidature, are essential for success.

MEXICAN AMERICAN PRIDE
PRINCIPLE NUMBER 8

> I will always support and protect the rights
> of Mexican American and other Hispanics,
> including those of the undocumented.

 IN THIS SECTION WE EXPLORE AND DISCUSS ISSUES of legal and human rights that Mexican Americans and Hispanics confront in the United States and possible ways to solve them.

1. Mexican Americans and Hispanics of all origins share common traits and some differences.

2. Differences include the way they arrived in this country, their challenges, acceptance, treatment upon arrival and subsequent treatment as a group

3. Regardless of the way Hispanic Americans happen to be in this country we must unite to solve our problems here. We also need to present a unified front in looking after the welfare of the Latin American countries so that the need for emigration subsides.

4. Deportation and "Involuntary repatriation" of Mexicans and Mexican Americans has always been a recurrent feature of life in the United States.

5. In recent years deportations were supposed to be selective of criminals. In practice however, deportations are indiscriminate

and frequently involve people who have been in the country working and contributing to America for many years.

6. Forgotten victims of deportation are the children, who being United States citizens are sent to a country they do not know. On the other side, equally victimized, are the children, United States citizens who have been left alone in this country without parents after their parents were deported. An urgent well-structured program for care of these children, United States citizens, is needed.

7. Mexican American lives have improved, but there is still much to be done. Their further improvement depends on many needed accomplishments listed as the objectives cited in this Mexican American Pride book.

8. Improvement of the lives of migrant agricultural workers and unskilled laborers is necessary as key indicators of Mexican American Progress.

9. Mexican American and Hispanic organizations are effective at working in defense and for the progress of Mexican Americans and Hispanics. Speakers for these organizations should act quickly, be more energetic, and direct when Mexican American and Hispanics need support or are attacked.

10. Hispanics should unify their efforts for Hispanics to be successful in this country. Differences between the groups, whatever they may be, should be ironed out. If we act in unison, there is nothing we cannot accomplish.

11. We need to act together to resolve the issue of immigration and pass immigration and refugee legislation.

Hispanics have much in common including language and customs. On the other hand, there are some differences which are minor such as food preferences that make for a pleasant variety. Celebrations of national origin such as music and festivities serve as bonds, not only among Hispanics but also with the rest of Americans. Other differences are major, the greatest being how they became residents or citizens of the United States.

Mexican Americans are the largest of the Hispanic groups in the United States. Some Mexican Americans trace their origin to the time when the southwest was part of Mexico. Many more came to the United States in the period between the end of the Mexican American war and 1924 when becoming a resident of the United States was as simple as crossing the border and paying a small fee. The highest immigration during that time was related to revolutions and uprisings in Mexico and to peaks in labor needs such as the gold rush in California, mining and oil exploitation. The Second World War required Mexican labor and gave origin to the Bracero Program. Many Mexicans stayed in the country, eventually became legal residents and raised children here who were citizens by birth. There were repatriations of Mexicans, voluntary as well as forced. The largest repatriation took place during the Great Depression when Mexican Americans were denied work as long as "real Americans" were unemployed.

Repatriation during the depression year was carried out illegally but with support of the federal state and local governments. At times repatriation was given the aura of being voluntary but arose out of intimidation tactics. Mexican and Mexican Americans not only were denied the opportunity to work but were forcibly removed from their homes without being allowed to take care of their property and belongings. Included in these massive deportations were legal residents as well as American citizens by birth. These deportations were not the only ones to occur in the history of this country; unfortunately, they are still occurring and will continue to take place because the authorities are able to prey on Mexican Americans with impunity.

Deportation of undocumented Mexicans continues to this day. Is often said that only undocumented Mexicans with criminal records are deported. The truth is much different. Most deportees do not have criminal records, and those who do are people that have been stopped by police in instances of outright illegal profiling. It is well known that the undocumented out of fear avoid contact with police even when they themselves are the victims of crime. It is also well known that the undocumented statistically commit real criminal acts at an extremely low rate compared to statistics for the rest of the population.

Deportation of the undocumented often involves men and women who have led productive lives here for many years even decades. These longtime residents, both men and women, when deported often leave children who are in this way orphaned. Most of these children in fact are American citizens by birth. There is no clearly structured system for the care of children when their parents are deported. Some states allow undocumented parents to designate "standby" guardians in case they are deported. Most of the ICE orphaned children are taken care by other undocumented families compounding the problem. An urgent well-structured program providing for taking care of this children is badly needed.

Ignored by nearly all is the tragedy of school age children who are deported to Mexico along with their parents. Many, are American citizens by birth equally tragic in most cases is the faith of the ICE orphaned children who are left in the United States after the parents are deported, most of them American Citizens. As of 2016 an estimated half a million children with United States citizenship were enrolled in Mexican schools. The number of children left without parents in the United States was estimated to number 5.9 million in an article published in Time magazine in March 2018 The children of these two groups struggle to complete their studies and many do not and thus are lost. Their bilingualism could be an asset to both countries and yet the way they are treated is a waste in human resources for both countries. Mexican authorities should make it easier for these students to enroll in Mexican schools. American authorities should make sure that the children left without parents in the United States complete their education.

The lives of the undocumented Mexicans along with those of the Mexican Americans have been much less than an "American Dream." They were for years cheated, robbed, killed and lynched by European Americans. All those years and until after the Second World War they were discriminated against and victimized by sanctioned government practices. For the next sixty years from the 1950s until the end of the twentieth century their lives did not improve much. Since the beginning of the twenty-first century (in the last twenty years) their lives began to change and it finally looks like Mexican Americans are ready to join the rest of Americans in a better more satisfying more productive life. The change has been and is happening because of better education and because Mexican Americans have started to improve their own lives by serving in community affairs and governance.

Much remains to be done to improve Mexican American lives. Their further advancement is linked to the improvement the lives of undocumented Mexican workers, migrant farmworkers and workers in other menial and indispensable jobs which are the life line of the nation. More action is needed to protests and defend the victims of deportation. Unlike black leaders who defend African Americans, Mexican American leaders for the most part are silent and allow injustices to occur with only token efforts to fight them. When Texas, Arizona, Oklahoma, other states and individual communities enact laws that effectively target Hispanics in obvious racial profiling, legal challenges on the base of constitutionality are slow and for many too late to help with the utter disruption of their lives.

LULAC, MALDEF, and LA RAZA respected Hispanic and Mexican American organizations should and must act without delay and with effectiveness in defense. Individually or as a group these organizations must have a rapid deployment corps that is charged with directing such defense. That defense must be readily apparent, energetic and done in such way as to neutralize the fear mongering of racist groups. These groups, frequently white supremacists, arouse pseudo patriotic feelings among the American public to disguise their anti-Mexican American and anti-Hispanic attitudes. Mexican American and Hispanic individuals in position of responsibility and authority must act in defense of Mexican American and Hispanic citizens who are singled out for possible deportation. Unfortunately, Mexican Americans lack well-spoken and willing leaders who could act in a rapid response fashion when the occasion requires it. No Mexican American or Hispanic citizen should be questioned about his or her legal status in the country any more than any European American, to do otherwise is racial profiling, therefore unconstitutional and must be resisted by all individuals and Hispanic organizations.

Puerto Ricans constitute the second largest Hispanic group in the United States. Puerto Ricans are American citizens by virtue of Puerto Rico being a Commonwealth associate of the United States. Many Puerto Ricans have attained recognition and fame in this country, but for the most part Puerto Ricans share the poverty and low educational status of Mexican Americans and other Hispanic groups. Stateside Puerto Ricans have become more numerous than those living in Puerto Rico. Being American citizens by virtue of the special relationship with the United States they are free to migrate into this country. Even though they are American citizens they are still faced with discriminatory attitudes.

Cuban Americans and Cuban immigrants have distinct advantages when migrating to the United States. Most of the Cuban people that originally came to the United States after Castro's revolution were people of certain means. They were doctors, engineers, well educated, upper class and able to start a new life in the United States with relative ease. Those early immigrants were helped to settle in this country by legislation that provided economic help for them. Immigrants coming later were and are still relatively well received, considered refugees persecuted in Cuba for political reasons.

Cubans have made great strides in this country and have taken care of themselves quite well. They have improved Miami and southern Florida and are influential in commerce and politics not only in Florida where most Cubans locate, but throughout the United States. Cubans are fun loving, likable people, industrious, and in a way, they have taken over wherever they have chosen to live. They help each other to succeed and, in many ways, they are an example to the other Hispanic groups. For the most part, Cubans and Cuban Americans have not had the same experience as Mexican Americans or Puerto Ricans have had, living under repressive discriminatory conditions in the United States. Politically, Cuban Americans are aligned with the Republican Party and regrettably their congressional representatives decided to separate from the Hispanic Congressional Caucus weakening this organization.

If indeed Cuban and Cuban Americans have adapted well and progressed and thrived in this country there is a big obstacle for the complete enjoyment of their success. The most regrettable aspect of the otherwise successful American Experience is their political alliance with the Republican Party which is committed to making Cuba and Cubans suffer for defying American Hegemony in the hemisphere. It just does not make sense that after sixty years United States is still penalizing Cuba when they have such relations with its former terrible enemies. Namely Japan, Vietnam, North Korea, and Germany.

There has to be a solution to the situation of Cuban American relations. When Obama was president there was a ray of hope that the situation would improve but the Trump passion for undoing any progressive Obama accomplishment sealed its fate. This was an obvious concession to the Cuban American old guard. One would hope for the sake of all Cubans and indeed all Latin American Nations that this state of utterly animosity would pass. Successful Cuban Americans would be much better off if they invested in Cuba, traveled to Cuba and helped Cuba. Because of the character of her people Cuba has great potential and we all hope that that potential becomes a reality.

Salvadoran immigrants are estimated to be the fourth largest Hispanic group in the United States closely followed by Dominicans and people identifying themselves as of Spanish descent. Other numerically significant groups are Guatemalan, Colombian, Peruvian, Honduran and Nicaraguan. Population estimates in the United States of Hispanics from other Latin-American nations including Brazil, Argentina and Chile are much lower but significant when in aggregate. The immigrant population of the northern triangle nations of Central America is increasing rapidly because of violence, crime, poverty and climatic conditions that make their agricultural production insufficient to. provide sustenance.

The dire conditions in which Central Americans live now need bold steps for correction. Allowing emigration to reach diaspora levels is not the answer. There is no question that people want and actually love to live in their own country with their own people if conditions are favorable. Such favorable conditions are not there. Several possible solutions to the Central American migration have been discussed in terms of the need to provide jobs for the residents in the area. One is the creation of a commercial trade market with Southern Mexico that establishes work centers in the three nations. Several sources in this country have mention the need for the United States to invest in the area with the same objective. Crime and violence are more difficult problems to control such as is the situation in Mexico. The drug traffic and common criminality associated with drug traffic are vexing problems whose solution is difficult to envision without the use of military force that brings with it inescapably claims of human rights violations.

Migration from Dominican Republic and Colombia has been stimulated by both economic and instability factors. Revolutions in Salvador, Guatemala and Nicaragua, natural disasters in Honduras and strife in Venezuela and Colombia were and are powerful factors in large migrations from those countries. Brazilian migration has also been significant. Hispanics from those countries tend to migrate to areas already populated by other Hispanic groups. Greatest concentration of Hispanics is therefore in the southwestern states, Gulf coast and northeastern United States as well as in larger cities elsewhere. In the later year's significant dispersion of Hispanic population has taken place to almost every state of the union mostly in response to labor needs.

Whatever their national origin and their reasons for residing in the United States Hispanics need to try to overcome their respective differences and unify their efforts. This unification of efforts is needed in order to succeed in every meaningful aspect of life in this country. As a group, and with little differences within, Hispanics are disrespected as individuals and as an ethnic group. In recent years and in great part due to the illegal immigration problem, all Hispanics have become victims of disparaging comments, discriminatory practices and even physical attacks by hate groups spurred on by reactionary, hysterical, and militant white supremacist talk The careless anti-Mexican and anti-Mexican American attitude of President Trump has further escalated the violence resulting in the El Paso terrorist attack. There is no doubt that President Trump is largely responsible for that attack. The President in his need to cater to white supremacist support to be re-elected has shown no remorse for the attack and no change in attitude.

Undocumented immigration is a large problem that needs resolution. The 9/11 attack brought greater awareness to the illegal immigrant population in the United States, even though the terrorists who carried out the attack were legally admitted to this country. The porosity of United States borders is a problem that needs particular attention. Certainly, nations have the right to control their borders and regulate immigration. Absolute control of the borders of this country is a formidable and perhaps impossible task. Illegal immigration is greater through the southern, Mexican border even though illegal entry here is more difficult than through the northern, Canadian border. The Canadian border is longer and considerably less guarded. One would think that the more relaxed security of this border together with the makeup of the Canadian population that includes many Middle Easterners would make easier point for terrorists to cross into this country. However, this seems to be of no concern presently.

Illegal immigration also takes place through overstaying visitors or individuals granted temporary admission for work or as tourists overstaying their permitted time. It is fair to say that the terrorist threat represented by illegal Hispanic immigrants is nonexistent. The overwhelming majority of them migrate only to find work in order to provide for their families back home. It is also fair and accurate to say that determined terrorists will find a way to carry out their acts, given the impossibility of absolutely controlling immigration and control of transportation means entering the country. Any further terrorist act in this country will more than likely be carried out by individuals legally admitted to the country, who are provided with weapons or devices that have entered in uninspected transportation conveyances. Any terrorist-minded individual or group would be well advised to enter legally or illegally through the Canadian border where immigration is much easier rather than through the inhospitable and much more challenging southern Mexican border. Nevertheless, it is imperative for the United States to control its borders.

Controlling borders is going to be an extremely difficult to even impossible task unless a rational immigration policy is put in place. A rational immigration policy should include a program for temporary admission of needed workers and a resolution of the status of the many undocumented residents already here. The United States depends greatly on the work of immigrants. They perform work that most Americans, particularly European Americans, prefer not to do. Their work also allows Americans to perform more productive, better paid and meaningful jobs. Properly managed, a temporary guest worker program could resolve the needs of the immigrants and of our nation. The need of the immigrants arises from the poor conditions in their respective countries. The United States needs reliable low-paid workers who are willing to work seasonally and go back to their countries after completion of their contracts. It is fair to say that most Mexican, Central American, and other Hispanic temporary workers would be happy to go back home if a legal means for renewable contracts for temporary work would be available. Presently the life of an illegal Hispanic immigrant is extremely difficult. They fear deportation, they fear being victims of crime without the protection or help from authorities. Income tax is withheld from their wages for the coffers of the nation that cannot be claimed back and are cheated of their pay because they do not dare to complain.

Illegal immigration can best be resolved through a comprehensive approach that includes border control, regularization of the current illegal immigrant population allowing them the opportunity to become legal residents and in particular by the formulation of a guest worker program. The longer the federal government takes to develop a comprehensive approach to immigration the more chaotic the situation becomes. Individual states and communities taking their own approach of punishing illegal immigrants makes the problem worse by affecting the entire Hispanic population and the individual state's economy. Piecemeal measures taken by some states, communities or individuals simply are not enough and only cause harm to all Hispanics and to the country. Putting up a border wall may slow down but certainly will not stop illegal immigrants who defy all obstacles to come to this country.

This new Iron Curtain proposed by Trump is going to be breached much more easily than the one the Russians built to deter Eastern Europeans who wanted to defect to the west and its opportunities. Much as we like to think that the Eastern European motive to defect was democracy and freedom, the real reason was the opportunity to improve their income and obtain the essential goods for a better quality of life. That is precisely the reasons illegal immigration occurs not only to The United States but the European Union, Russia, South Korea, Australia, and even China.

There is also illegal immigration to Mexico, Argentina, Brazil, Cuba, and the Dominican Republic and almost in any country where people can make a better living than in their own. That is the reason why Hispanic illegal immigrants come to this country, not terrorist intentions; not freedom and democracy because here they are not free but fearful; not healthcare, because illegal immigrants fear to expose themselves and be found out; not the welfare, not education for their children; but simply for the opportunity to work at low-paying jobs to provide food and a little comfort to their families back home. In their quest, defying danger, bandits, corrupt police, coyotes, abuse, possible loss of limbs and even loss of life will not stop them. And a little wall by comparison with the other obstacles they face to get here will not stop them. They will dig under it, climb over it, make a hole in it or whatever it takes, but they will break through. Deport them and the next day, next week or next month they will be back because they need to. "Aqui estamos, no nos vamos y si nos echan regresamos." "We are here, we will not leave, and if they throw us out, we will come back." That is their cry that is their quest.

As Hispanics we can understand why our people come to this country, legally and illegally. Their reasons to come here are not different from the reasons Europeans come. We must unite and fight for our freedom as American citizens and for the legitimate hopes and dreams of the undocumented. We all share a Hispanic and Latin American heritage and must work together for recognition and justice. America needs us and we must be prepared to contribute to this nation's well-being and prosperity.

One way for Hispanics to demonstrate our unity and solidarity with our people is to vote in any election only for candidates who support our needs. Hispanics should oppose and vote against those candidates who are against immigration, against those who only want so-called secure borders and instead vote and work for the election and campaign effort of those candidates that promote comprehensive immigration reform.

The last effort to pass a comprehensive immigration bill was defeated by a strong and organized anti-immigration campaign. Those individuals and groups overwhelmed the Senate with anti-immigrant emails, letters, and phone calls and scared the legislators with promises of defeat if they were to vote for adoption of the immigration bill. The comprehensive immigration bill was attacked with anti-immigrant comments and supported with only few comments in favor. The result was that the immigration reform bill was not brought to a vote despite the previous favorable sentiments. The bill apparently had enough support by Republic Senators to pass but a few Democratic Senators fearful of losing their seat withheld their support. Next time that a comprehensive immigration bill is presented and comes for discussion in the Senate and in the House, Hispanic individuals and organizations must be ready to mount a massive pro-immigration reform campaign of letters, email, and phone calls to their Senators and Representatives. Mexican Americans and Hispanics must learn to communicate with their legislators. It is up to the Hispanic organizations to lead in this effort and is up to all of us to support it with our vote. In addition to voting it will be highly useful for all of us to communicate with our representatives early and often.

MEXICAN AMERICAN PRIDE
PRINCIPLE NUMBER 9

> I will support Mexican American and other Hispanics
> as candidates for public office, but I will
> demand performance and honesty from them.

 IN THIS CHAPTER WE DISCUSS THE FOLLOWING:

1. The status of Hispanic people after Obama presidency. The ascendency of the black American people versus the relative invisibility of Hispanic and Mexican Americans.

2. The need for Mexican American and Hispanic organizations to be more vocal and timely helping victims of aggressive discriminatory and cruel actions.

3. We need to develop individuals who can openly speak in defense of Mexican Americans.

4. We need to make a reality the potential of Mexican American and Hispanic political strength.

5. We have to coordinate the decisions and activities of all Hispanic groups to obtain a mutual objective of benefit to all Hispanics.

6. We need to elect effective and honest Mexican American and Hispanics to political positions of authority.

7. We need to have Mexican American and Hispanics guide the country in the direction of a sensible and profitable relation with Latin America.

It is essential for Mexican Americans and Hispanics to share in the power that public office brings to various groups within the national community. The number of Mexican American public office holders is very low in proportion to the size of the Mexican American population. The same is true for most of the other Hispanic national groups, except for Cuban Americans who seem to have attained a degree of parity with European American groups. After Obama was elected and became the first black President of the United States, Hispanics can no longer claim discrimination as the barrier to performance in public affairs. In large part because of the undocumented immigration problem which has been exclusively focused on Hispanics, particularly on Mexicans the anti-Hispanic and anti-Mexican groups are trying and succeeding in discrediting all that represents Hispanic. That in fact, has made Hispanics the new favorite group target of discrimination, replacing African Americans who will not take it anymore.

The change in attitude of the American public towards blacks can be seen everywhere. It can be seen in sports, television programming, movies and other broadcasting services. At the same time however, Hispanics are hardly ever seen in the English-speaking media. Spanish programming has increased but mostly on Spanish-speaking services. This situation is symptomatic of the low participation of Mexican Americans in public discourse and indicates that Mexican Americans need to become more involved in the public arena. Mexican American and Hispanic organizations need to speak more loudly when the needs and complaints of Mexican Americans and Hispanics are ignored. We need vigorous, well-spoken, inspiring Mexican American individuals to be the first responders when situations arise. Too often the people defending Mexican Americans are not Hispanics. It is great that people like Beto O'Rourke comes forcibly to the defense of injured Mexican and Mexican American people in El Paso, but he is not Mexican American nor Hispanic. Where are our leaders? We need a new Cesar

Chavez, Dolores Huerta, or we need a louder Julian Castro, Joaquin Castro, maybe Henry Cisneros? Or a new Cisneros? How about if Ruben Navarrette, who seems to be a great writer, would put aside his pen for a while and takes the podium? How about Alfredo Corchado who loves his homelands? He must be a very good speaker having written such a great book where he opens his heart. We need someone or "someones" with a strong voice and no fear to come out and make the Mexican American voice heard.

Support for Hispanic issues and defense of Hispanics against discriminatory and abusive practices require leaders to mount a strong and appropriate response. All Hispanic American citizens regardless of country of origin and whether they were born in this country or not, must be ready to counter the forces of intolerance. They must support their leaders and present a unified front.

Statistically, Mexican Americans and Hispanics are becoming a sizeable political force. Their theoretical political force needs to become real; it needs to be nourished. The necessary nourishment lies in inducing Hispanic legal residents to become American citizens, those who are citizens to vote in every single election, support its candidates and those who are able to run for office, to do so. Mexican Americans and Hispanics are present in large number in several states where they represent a significant percentage of the population. In Texas and California, they represent over 30% of the population. In Arizona, New Mexico, and Nevada they are over 20% of the population. Actually, the number of Mexican Americans and Hispanics may be underestimated because of the phenomenon of ethnic attrition. Ethnic attrition occurs through intermarriage and assimilation when in generation after generation the ethnic association and recognition progressively disappears. Everywhere Mexican Americans reside voting is important but more so in states and cities where they are numerous because there, they could more easily win elections for their candidates.

In regards to ethnic attrition it is recognized than both Hispanic and Mexican Americans marry non-Hispanic whites about 25% of the time. The children of these marriages progressively lose their Hispanic self- designation. Many of the members of those generations tend to do better economically and socially therefore often tending to be members of the Republican Party. It is extremely important that the members of later generations realize than in order for Mexican Americans and Hispanic to succeed we need our lower standing nonskilled workers to be pulled out of the dire conditions in which they are often victimized.

Regardless of political affiliation, Mexican American and Hispanics including those whose ties have been diluted through ethnic attrition need to vote with unity for any and all Hispanic candidates for public office when opposed by non-Hispanics. This may seem a harsh and undemocratic statement, but progress will not occur otherwise. Progress of all Mexican Americans demands that all Mexican Americans, including those highly successful and fortunate, stand in unity for the redemption of our people.

If it is the duty of Hispanics to elect Hispanic candidates, it is the duty of Hispanic office holders to perform their duties with efficiency and honesty. Both, Hispanic officials and Hispanic citizens have the inescapable duty to take responsibility for their actions as good American citizens and for being good, honest and responsible Mexican Americans and Hispanics. Our Hispanic legislators must get their act together. The Hispanic Congregational Caucus should act together to support Hispanic issues regardless of party affiliation. The Hispanic legislators have to act together in a single caucus for the advancement of Hispanics, putting aside party jalousies and party politics. They have a greater duty that partisan squabbles will not honor.

Unfortunately, the image of Mexican American and Hispanic public servants has at times been publicly and loudly tainted. At times they have been the target of political maneuvering but at other times the criticism and charges appear to be justified. It is imperative that the negative image of any Hispanic elected or appointed official be improved. This can be accomplished by Hispanics being vigilant and demand honesty and performance when negative facts or comments surface. In the Rio Grande Valley one of the disturbing political maneuvers is the use of politiqueras. Politiqueras is a word loosely translated as voter's assistants applies to persons (usually women) who go from door to door in a community helping residents to register to vote or helping with mail-in voting. This appears to be a helpful function and it is, except that sometimes Politiqueras have been known to sell votes. Obviously politiqueras' skill if properly carried out would serve an excellent and democratic political purpose.

At the same time, it is extremely important that all Hispanics come to the defense and support of Hispanic officials when charges are unfounded. Choose the candidates you support and once you do, work for their election. If there is no Hispanic candidate for an office, find one and convince him or her to run. Volunteer yourself if you are able to do so. Do not be a political party loyalist, unless you know that the candidate chosen by the party believes in the Hispanic cause, in addition to being good for America. Neither the Republican nor the Democratic Party is consistently a good choice for Hispanics. Be familiar with the issues candidates support, and let their views on Hispanic issues be your guide.

Hispanics must stand together in order to make a reality of the political force that so far remains mostly a potential. This is not only important for Hispanics living in the United States but for all Latin Americans everywhere, and more importantly for the benefit of the United States. For too long the United States has looked to Europe for relationships, commercial and otherwise; ignoring the potential Latin America offers as a true partner for progress. It is almost as if the United States were a European nation. In the last twenty years United States has strengthened commercial relationships with Asian countries while Latin American nations continue to be largely ignored. Empowering the Hispanic population of this country may result in the United States finally honoring the many promises that successive American presidents have made to Latin America. Those promises started with Franklin Delano Roosevelt in the dark days of the 1930s Great Depression and in the advent of the Second World War. The United States issued great protestations of friendship, unity and love to Latin America. Once the war was over the United States forgot the once promoted and hailed Americanism. The American eyes turned to Europe, embracing and supporting European friends and enemies and abandoning the hemispheric friends and allies.

There always were, and there are now, great opportunities for profit and mutual benefits in this continent. Latin America is still an underdeveloped area with great natural resources and great potential in its large but as yet poorly productive population. American investment and American know how could lift the area and transport it into the twenty-first century, producing amazing mutual progress and benefits. The rise of Hispanic political power here could see us leading the American initiatives and making a Pan American partnership possible. Hispanic political power could persuade other Americans move the rest of Americans to think differently about Latin America and would allay the amply justified distrust Latin Americans have, of the United States' intentions.

This is no time to become disappointed in America. President Trump has made bad decisions. The Republican Party, which controls the Senate, seems incapable of opposing his poor decisions. The abandonment and criticism of our European friends, Trumps friendship with world despots, denial of climate change and the withdrawal from the Iran nuclear deal are regrettable. The country is greatly divided and is a little battered, mainly by poor judgment and unwise strategic decisions on the part of Trump and the politicians entrusted with our government. But the country is strong and full of possibilities. Hispanics have the opportunity to actively participate in a national renewal of faith in our government and progress. For this, we Hispanics have to work a lot harder in the task of realizing our potential. We must improve our education, our behavior and our American citizenship.

MEXICAN AMERICAN PRIDE
PRINCIPLE NUMBER 10

> I will demand respect for my human rights
> and the rights of all other racial and national groups.

1. Declaration of the human rights throughout history

2. The impact of the United States Declaration of Independence.

3. Human rights in the United States.

4. Black Americans' struggles against discrimination and for freedom, equality, and social justice.

5. Persistent inequality of minorities and discriminatory practices against them despite recent and unsuccessful efforts to improve their rights.

6. The irony of our United States government officials proclaiming the expansion of democracy and human rights around the world while ignoring and trampling over those principles at home.

7. The destructive and grievous assaults of anti-Mexican American, anti-Hispanic, anti-immigrant of white supremacists' organizations.

8. The tolerance of and even encouragement of human rights vi-
    olations in the United States.

9. The progress of Mexican Americans and Hispanics in their ef-
    forts to enjoy the principles of the Universal Declaration of
    Human Rights.

10. The continuing struggle of black American organizations and
    the need for Hispanic organizations to be more proactive in de-
    fending against anti Mexican-American and Anti-Hispanic acts.

11. The need to promote human rights and prosperity among all
    American nations and the role of Hispanics to promote this
    ideal.

The concept of human rights has evolved through the centuries from the democratic principles of Greece and Rome to the United Nations Universal Declarations of Human Rights. Significant steps in this evolution were the Magna Carta, the Declaration of Independence of United States, and the French Revolutions' Declaration of the Rights of Man and of the Citizen.

The Universal Declaration of Human Rights by the United Nations (UN) was preceded by similar declaration of the Organization of American States (OAS) that included not only human rights but also human duties.

The thirty Articles included in the United Nations Declaration and the thirty-eight rights and duties expressed in the similar OAS document are too many to discuss in detail. This chapter will discuss only those human rights that more often are violated to the detriment of Hispanics.

Article one of the OAS and Article 3 of the UN Human Rights declarations speak of the rights of human beings to life, liberty and personal security. These statements may have very well inspired in the United States declaration of independence from England:

> We hold these truths to be self-evident, that all men are cre-
> ated equal, that they are endowed by the Creator with certain

unalienable Rights that among these are Life, Liberty, and the pursuit of Happiness.

The problem with that wonderful and powerful statement is that it did not include men other than white men. In other words, the statement did not apply to blacks, Indians, or any colored race. The statement did not apply to women either. Life and liberty of course did not apply to blacks most of whom continuing being slaves. The signatories of the articles of independence themselves were slave owners. Life and liberty did not apply to Indians who were killed and tortured by the thousand and dispossessed of their lands even following treaties that were never respected. Years later Mexican Americans were treated in similar way, dispossessed of their lands, killed and placed in a state of near servitude. That near servitude status continues to this date in the fields of Texas, California and elsewhere.

Things have improved significantly from the darkest days, thanks mostly to African Americans sacrifices and activism and to those of their leaders, namely: Martin Luther King and his followers. It is fair to say that black American leaders of today are much more active and involved in defending and promoting black American causes and individuals, than similar Hispanic leaders. Black American leaders can put the fear of God into white racists while Hispanic leaders seem to only provoke pity, at best. As a consequence of this lack of true leadership Mexican-Americans and Hispanics in general have become the selected people to discriminate.

The right of freedom is still out of sight for Hispanic and black Americans. They are by far the largest portion of the jail population in this country, which in turn has the largest proportion of jailed population than any other western country. While roughly one in 150 Americans is in jail, one out of fourteen black males and one in twenty-seven Hispanics males are in jail. For the United States, this is a phenomenal loss of potentially gainful workers, A painful los to families, painful to the children who grow up fatherless and to the wives or partners who are converted into single parents, perhaps for life. This is an unspeakable crime against human rights. It is especially a crime directed to children as they grow without role model in an environment of poverty, lawlessness and crime.

Recently, there have been efforts to change our justice system and policing practices. Drug arrests especially for small amount of marihuana and for minor crimes have decreased. Many states have passed permissive laws for drug possession. Governments had little choice after an increasing number of states have approved medical use of marihuana and some even for recreational use. Incarceration laws in some states have been made more moderate in some states after the "Three arrests and you are out" disaster. That catchy phrase had the effect of increasing our already phenomenal incarceration rate. It also further enriched the "for profit" jailing business that are only too happy to oblige, building larger, tougher but not better jails. Policing practices have also changed some for the better. Changes and demonstration of such as techniques using de-escalation lecturing in the better use of policing have been helpful. Demonstration on how to interpret defensive behavior of psychiatric patients and people under stress has also helped.

In summary in spite of the helpful signs, it is fair and accurate to say that there is no Freedom and Equality before the law and for far too many Black and Hispanics Americans no Equal opportunities to pursue and attain Happiness (Capital letters intended.) Life is still an unsure Right for so many of our people. The United States government frequently accuses other countries of Human Rights violations but fails for the most part to recognize its own Crimes against Humanity. Still, our government officials have the temerity to go around the world proclaiming our intention to promote democracy, freedom, human rights, woman's rights, religious and speech rights.

Broadcasters at Fox News encourage discrimination and indirectly even violence, against Hispanics repeating Trump's "Hispanic invasion," "Criminal illegal immigrants," and similar Trump's favorite phraseology to refer to Mexican Americans and Hispanics. The anti-Hispanic sentiment generated by these network broadcasters spreads easily to otherwise well-meaning European Americans. It is time that we, as Hispanics bring our growing purchasing power to bear on these networks by refusing to buy from the advertisers supporting such programming. Our Hispanic leaders have to learn the skills and acquire the means necessary to excite, unite and move our people and to forcibly discuss issues in defense of our Hispanic culture and our rights.

Article seven of the UN declaration of human rights deals about the right of equality before the law, equal protection against any discrimination and against incitement to discrimination. So where is the protection against the offending networks and against groups such as the Minuteman and other vigilante groups that make it their mission to harass Hispanics? It is not only undocumented Hispanics that are subject to discrimination and violence encouraged against. These actions are also taken against legal Mexican and Hispanic immigrants and Mexican and Hispanic United States citizens.

The Minuteman Project is a special case. The group portrays itself to be against illegal immigration but in reality, their motive is to preserve the "American way of life" as they interpret it, that is a society for white European Americans, enjoying cheap (inexpensive) servants who have no civil rights. The resemblance to the KKK is not coincidental. These are the same people who at a different time had a different target, with the same objectives, smarter in their approach and more realistic in their aims. They wrap themselves in the American flag instead of the Confederate flag. They seem to convince some well-meaning white folks while attracting the white supremacists, who form the core of the group.

We as a united Hispanic family must take steps to achieve a culture of acceptance from the rest of the American society. First of all, we must accept and practice the concepts outlined in the Mexican American pride principles. The same principles apply to all Hispanics. These are the steps that we must take to aspire to be accepted as true Americans. The way will not be easy; it will be painful and long. When we finally achieve it, after enduring years and indeed centuries of being treated as second class citizens and worse, we will be truly proud Americans.

Besides taking the steps to be good American citizens, we must defend our rights as free people. To do that, we must act against individuals, groups and corporations that encourage acts and positions against our language, our culture and our heritage. On the other hand, we must support those who support our aspirations. We must participate in public events as free Americans and endure sacrifices. African Americans had to fight, suffer and die before they could achieve some acceptance by white society; acceptance that also still is, in large part based on fear. That is why their leaders still appear wherever there is an obvious anti-black act. Obviously, the measure of their acceptance as equal citizens has to be still defended and protected. Women as a group also have to fight, and continue fighting for their rights. Their fight for their reproductive rights and for equal pay for equal work continues. We as Hispanics cannot gain our rights by riding on the backs of African Americans or rely on the women's rights successes. We must endure our own struggle and fight our own battles.

The Southern Christian Leadership Conference (SCLC) and the National Association for Advancement of Colored People (NAACP) were instrumental in ending segregation in the south and lessening discrimination throughout the United States. These associations, with the help of rights groups and the strong backing of president Johnson did an excellent job and continue to do so. Their efforts need to be continued for the foreseeable future. Even now, after a black American president the labors of the NAACP are not finished. Racial intolerance is not dead; it is being fueled every day by racist people who with the pretext of protecting America and "the American way of life" incite otherwise well-meaning people to side with them. This time the intolerance and discrimination are directed mainly towards Hispanics.

Discrimination against Hispanics is nothing new, it has been there all the time, the same discriminatory tactics used against blacks were, and are still directed towards Hispanics. The difference now, is that blacks will not take it anymore while Hispanics are divided and effectively unorganized.

Hispanics have associations that have tried to defend our rights, regrettably with only limited success. Their efforts are not nearly as successful as those of the SCLC and the NAACP, perhaps in part because Hispanic leaders are not as aggressive or forceful in their opinions and arguments. The main Hispanic defense organizations are LULAC (League of United Latin American Citizens), MALDEF (Mexican American Defense League) and NCLR (National Council of La Raza, now Unidos US). These organizations as well as the many other Hispanic organizations need to be strengthened with the support of all Hispanics. We need to strengthen those organizations so that they can better act to protect our human and civil rights.

These organizations assign themselves different missions but maybe they should get together to have a common arm that would functions similar to the NAACP. Such a body would react specifically in cases of discrimination against Mexican Americans and Hispanics and call on an immediate response team that mobilizes in cases like the El Paso massacre, also in police shooting of unarmed Hispanic civilians and in Anti-Hispanic demonstrations and violence. This body could come to defense in cases coming to Congress, the Supreme Court and in similar State government bodies.

Much progress has been obtained by Mexican Americans and Hispanics in the last seventy-five years and particularly in the last twenty. We have the support of most of the American people even though some resistance to our progress is still evident. Resistance is much in evidence in Trump's speeches and in the support that he receives in his campaign rallies.

It is not surprising that so many white people are nervous towards our ascendance in American society. They see the era of white people privileges ending. We must reassure them that we Mexican American and Hispanic American people are taking the banner of American successes and accomplishments and running with it. We will continue good relations with Europe, we will work closely with Asiatic nations and help African nations to a better future. We will work for peace in the Middle East and for a just world for all people. In addition, and importantly this time we will work with the rest of the Western Hemisphere nations for common peace, justice and prosperity. We will do this by improving communications, combating organized drug traffic and establishing active commercial and people to people relations. We in the United States must become knowledgeable and cooperate with all the nations of the western hemisphere.

One of the most important aims for the Western Hemisphere Nations is to strengthen the support and respect for human rights in every one of our countries. A most important objective is to improve the economy of Latin America so that every one of their inhabitants live with safety and comfort obviating the need to emigrate. We must rethink and renovate the idea of the Pan-American Highway. Perhaps it is time to think about an advanced Pan-American railway system. American nations need a Pan-American advanced terrestrial communication system that stimulates commerce, progress, prosperity and understanding among the American nations.

MEXICAN AMERICAN PRIDE
PRINCIPLE NUMBER 11

> I will oppose racial profiling when it is used
> in abuse of any person's rights.

 IN THIS CHAPTER WE WILL DISCUSS THE FOLLOWING CONCEPTUAL ISSUES:

1. The proper and improper use of racial profiling.

2. The great, almost universal occurrence of racial profiling of minorities by police in the United States is in fact a constant abuse of minority rights unequaled in the rest of the democratic world.

3. Arrests of minority members through the use of racial profiling is decreasing somewhat but still is much greater than the rate for non-Hispanic whites.

4. Racial profiling of Muslims is the new and largely unjustified act sanctioned by the Supreme Court of the United States.

5. Racial profiling of Mexican Americans in Arizona has been also been virtually sanctioned by the Supreme Court.

6. The Republican Party, unsure of maintaining a strong hold on the Mexican American population, is actively neutralizing the voting power of Mexican Americans through redistricting and voting suppression.

7. During the 2018 electoral campaign in Texas Mexican Americans began to realize the importance of their vote. More importantly the effort was highly dependent on young voters.

8. There are measures that victims of racial profile should take to minimize the impact of this practice.

9. Mexican Americans everywhere can profit from the near victory in the 2018 Texas Senatorial campaign.

10. Mexican Americans must act with unanimity in areas where they have large population density. Here they can show the importance of their voting power and of their commitment to the United States.

Racial profiling more broadly defined is the collection of racial or ethnic data to predict behavior. In some areas such as in medicine it can be useful, leading to a more personalized treatment with better results for the patient. Evidence show that some of the collected profile data can be used to provide medicine at different doses to different racial groups to achieve optimal treatment results. Other collected data show that different racial groups respond differently to a certain disease and that diseases are more frequent in certain groups.

The most objectionable aspect of racial profiling occurs when ethnic groups are singled out as suspects of criminal behavior, leading to unjustified police arrests and incarceration rates. Racial profiling for suspected criminal behavior is regrettably very common in the United States. It is well known that blacks and Hispanics are stopped by police while driving much more frequently than whites. When stopped they are also more likely than whites to have their cars searched. The reason for the search is usually because of suspected drug possession or trafficking or other criminal behavior. This fact alone accounts for the first arrest and frequently for the first conviction of blacks and Hispanics. In the worst cases drugs are planted to justify the arrest.

When blacks and Hispanics are brought to trial, they suffer from another profiling process. They more often than not, are provided with the worst defense, given the most severe and longest sentences and the fewest breaks. Once in jail they are lost to society. As previously discussed, jail often leads to a criminal career, jails being great schools for criminal behavior.

Such racial profile-initiated arrests more frequently occur in areas where whites are a majority of the population and in exclusive white areas. It is traditional for blacks to avoid driving in exclusive white areas particularly at night to avoid being stopped by police.

Recent statistics indicate that arrests for minor crimes have fallen significantly. It seems that in multiple localities the arrest rates are down over 50 % among Hispanics and at times over 60% among blacks. Still compared with non-Hispanic whites the arrests for Hispanics are nearly three times higher and for blacks over four times higher

After 9/11 a new racial profiling pattern has emerged: Muslims being chosen for frisking at airports or being denied access to their reserved flights. When a poll was conducted asking opinions about profiling and detention of Muslims a striking majority of those polled approved of the practice. Unfortunately, those agreeing with that opinion included both, blacks and Hispanics. The United States Supreme Court sanctioned and approved the Trump issued block of immigration and even visas to the citizens of several Muslim countries dismissing lower District Courts opinions.

Racial profiling of Hispanics has taken a new impetus after state legislatures in Arizona, Alabama, Mississippi, Georgia and South Carolina enacted laws that legalize profiling of Hispanic individuals. Often the pretext for introduction of such laws is defense of the United States from the incursion of illegal aliens. Other times, the reason for such laws is the expense to taxpayers of providing services to the undocumented. In Arizona a federal judge ruled that police can ask about immigration status when any traffic offense occurs. The point ignored is the obvious fact that authorities are going to ask about immigration status mostly or only when an individual looks Hispanic.

Sadly, the Department of Justice ignored the issue of Hispanic profiling implicit in such laws when representing the federal government in the case against the Arizona law before the Supreme Court. The Supreme Court of the nation also declined to discuss that aspect of the Arizona law. That the Supreme Court chose to ignore and overlook that aspect of the law should not be surprising, after all the Supreme Court accepted slavery for nearly one hundred years and accepted discrimination of blacks for two hundred years in this country which is supposed to be the beacon of democracy for the world.

The immigration law passed by Alabama is still most restrictive than Arizona. Alabama not only upheld requiring state and local authorities to inquire about immigration status after traffic stops or arrests but also barred the undocumented of applying or attending public universities. It also requires elementary and secondary schools to inquire immigration status of incoming students and voids any contracts if made with undocumented immigrants including for public services such as home water supply.

Profiling of Hispanics, citizens and not citizens, has also been one of the battle cries of the Tea Party and the Republican Party by extension, since the extreme right has taken hostage of the Republican Party. It is surprising that the Tea Party despite its anti-Hispanic stance is supported by some Hispanics. It should also be surprising that the anti-Hispanic Republican Party has complete control of the Texas government in a state where 40% of the population is Hispanic.

The reason for the domination of the Republic Party in Texas politics is actually not surprising. The reason is that few Hispanics, in particular extremely few Mexican Americans chose to vote and exercise their citizen's rights. In a recent past Mexican American voting in McAllen TX was an appalling 13%.

There is hope that Mexican Americans in Texas are awaking to the fact that that they need to increase their political involvement. Indeed, Mexican Americans in Southern Texas are acquiring American citizenship, increasing voter's registration and actually voting in increasing rates. There is increased involvement of the young Mexican Americans some of whom "cannot wait" to get involved.

The lessons of the 2018 electoral campaign must not be forgotten. Beto O'Rourke a non-Latin Candidate but still a Latino sympathizer with high energy and personal convictions. Beto with his Hispanicized first name was able to move and awake the Mexican American electorate especially the young voters who worked tirelessly for his election. Unfortunately, 2.1 million Hispanics most of them Mexican Americans failed to vote. If one tenth of them had voted, the opportunistic anti-Mexican American Senator Cruz would have been defeated. Let us not forget this important lesson. Mexican Americans had the opportunity to reject Cruz and avoid six more years of suffering, humiliation and victimization. The key is for all Mexican Americans to vote, including those who by homogenization and intermarriage are not 100% Mexican Americans anymore. We all need to vote.

Clearly racial profiling for suspected criminal behavior is wrong. People have the right to be treated equally and be treated as honest persons, innocent until proven guilty. In Texas the abuse of Mexican American Rights is at a new high. Mexican American parents in Texas are experiencing delays in receiving birth certificates for their newborns, an attempted denial of their American Citizenships. Mexican American citizens are being harassed; questioning their voting rights, questioning their right to driver's license and questioning their right to be issued passports.

With the pretext of need for increased militarization of the border Texas State Police have significantly increased their presence in Southern Texas. The police set road blocks in an obvious attempt to continue harassment and intimidation that are intimal parts of the Texas tradition of abuse of the Mexican American population.

Trying to keep absolute political power in Texas the Republican dominated legislature and the Texas Governor can now use the power of redistricting to diminish the impact of the potential Mexican American vote. Their machinations have been successful with the consent of a politically biased United States Supreme Court decision that failed to find their redistricting drawings unconstitutional.

The Republican Party in Texas is somewhat unsure if they will be able to maintain the present homogeneity of political power in the upcoming 2020 election and they are redoubling their efforts at voting suppression. Mexican Americans should be aware that a change of destiny is up to them through casting their vote. They must stop being the victims and turn into equal participants in American greatness.

Without being outright resistant citizens have the right to challenge unreasonable police orders. Challenge has to be done politely but firmly. Do not consent to have your auto searched if there is in your mind no reason to do so. If in spite of your good judgment the police go ahead and violate your right to refusal, take his or her name, police force of employment. and number. Complain to the corresponding authority and retain a lawyer if you can find one to take your case. If not, contact the American Civil Liberties Union about your case. If you feel that you have been detained purely because of racial profiling, complain to higher authorities.

Families in minority areas have the duty to stand for their youth. Organize and contact the police in your area. Seek cooperative relations between families and police organizations. Talk to your children; find out what is going on in their lives and keep them away from bad influences. The police will not reform their tough procedures on minorities unless we as parents do something to reform the system. Ending racial profiling as a predictor of criminal behavior is a priority that cannot be ignored. Talk to the mayor, talk to your local authorities, to your representative to your senator, to your governor Do not stay silent and give up on your children and their future.

To combat the kind of legalized Hispanic profiling as in the Arizona law is slightly more difficult. It requires Hispanic involvement in becoming citizens, voting, supporting organizations that defend Hispanic rights and choosing the right candidates to elect. It may also include taking a lesson from the black Americans in their defense of their civic rights and outright activism. The most important thing to remember that as in Texas in Arizona there is a large Mexican American population. The large population matters little if those who are able to become citizens do not, and if those who are citizens do not vote. Mexican Americans have to own up to their responsibility.

In 2018 the electoral experience in Texas gave very important lesson as to what can be done in those areas where Mexican Americans are numerically large and a significant percentage of the total population.

Mexican Americans: We all need to pull in the same direction. We need to energize everywhere we can. Texas, California, Arizona, New Mexico, Nevada, and also in Chicago, Detroit, Philadelphia, Nebraska, Utah, Oregon, and Washington. In many of those locations we will never acquire political power, but let the people there know that we are valuable, hardworking and good American Citizens.

MEXICAN AMERICAN PRIDE
PRINCIPLE NUMBER 12

I will always provide economic and moral support
for members of my family and I will strive
to become a role model to them.

IN THIS CHAPTER WE DISCUSSED THE FOLLOWING:

1. Parents are responsible for guidance of the family and their ultimate success.

2. The desirable and undesirable national behavioral characteristics of our reference countries.

3. The need to adopt the desirable and avoid the undesirable traits.

4. The positive and negative factors that determine success or failure in the guidance of a family.

A family needs direction and it is the duty and privilege of parents to provide it. The success of a family and indeed of the nation depends on how children are raised. The ethical principles and the expectations of success in life depend greatly on the leadership and moral guidance imparted by parents.

The greatest tragedy and, consequence of the high number of arrests and incarceration of Mexican Americans and Hispanic fathers are families with fatherless children. In the case of deportation of both father and mother, the children are effectively left orphaned. Those children are left without father, maybe without both father and mother. Those children are left without role models, without guidance, without protection often in a poor, crime infested environment. That is a waste of human resources and unforgivable high State crime.

There is certainly an innate drive and dedication in all individuals. The rate of success is much greater when parents support their children and the family not only economically but morally. Parents are needed to provide direction and establishing guidelines and parameters of behavior.

There are also innate characteristics and national traits that define a nation. Those characteristics and traits also influence the degree of success or failure of a nation. Those national traits are both positive and negative. Mexican American and Hispanic individuals and families as every other national and racial groups have their own positive and negative characteristics. It is not an exaggeration to say that Latin American nations both admire and fear the United States because of those, American national traits.

For Mexican Americans and Hispanics to succeed in this country we must adopt the positive American national traits and make them our own. At the same time, as Hispanics we must keep and enhance our own positive traits and diminished, neutralize or discard our undesirable traits.

Americans, English, Germans, Irish, Italian, French, Chinese, Korean and every other national group have their special traits that define their national character. Latin American countries have similarities and differences in their national characteristics.

The positive American characteristics that better define this country and its people are: Enterprise, invention, industry, dedication, drive, progressiveness, altruism, philanthropy and generosity. While those characteristics are also present in individual Mexicans and Hispanics, they do not define the national character of the Latin American nations.

Negative American national characteristics that Latin American nations dislike and fear are their national militaristic behavior, aggression, ambition and pride that borders in hubris. Other negatives are loose social and moral behavior, lack of family cohesion.

Positive Mexican characteristics that Mexican Americans share as well are: artistry, resourcefulness, family strength, friendliness, romanticism, spirit of sacrifice and love for country. Negative traits that we must work to overcome are: indolence, inconsistency, tolerance for disorder and corruption.

Everyone knows about the high rates of success among Jewish, Korean, Hindus, Chinese and other groups in this country. Unfortunately, we also know the inadequate performance of so many Mexican Americans and other Hispanics.

There is no time to lose; we Mexican Americans have already harmed ourselves and our families by standing idly while living in this country of opportunity. We must shake free of our harmful traits, keep the good ones and become proud Mexican Americans and better than that, we must become proud Americans of Mexican descent.

In order for Mexican American children to succeed, parents have to become involved in their progress and development both physical and intellectual. If possible, parents should get involved in school activities and at least attend parent-teacher conferences, supervise and help with homework and follow-up their progress. High school graduation no longer guarantees a satisfactory job but lack of a high school diploma nearly always guarantees failure in life. In fact, in this era of automation, computerization and artificial intelligence, jobs require college education as a minimum. We have to meet that challenge

Education, with a professional or at least a bachelor's degree must now be the minimum objective sought. At a very minimum a trade school degree must be acquired to be able to sustain a successful life experience.

We have dealt in the second chapter of this book with the issue of education. And we have said that despite all the problems there are hopeful signs. The future will be brighter if we do our job.

Dealing with our negative traits is a difficult problem but the only thing required is firmness of purpose. Mexican Americans are not indolent,

Mexican Americans love pretty houses with pretty gardens. Years of frustration and boredom that have made it seem as though lack of progress is normal. Life in the colonias, the frustrations of dealing with the same problems year after year have become normal. So are no paved roads, no services, school bus not making it, floods when it rains. Life in cities with the same intolerable, frustrating conditions as in the colonias is somewhat accepted. Just like abuse, death, loss of what was your possessions, your family, your cattle to a superior, demanding tough white man or to a member of the Texas Rangers was accepted in the old days. Tolerance for the frustrating conditions have to stop. Colonias sometimes surge away from these conditions and become livable areas. Cities and towns in the Rio Grande Valley have become thriving clean and prosperous communities. Poor, unlivable, frustrating colonias and the unsafe, slum areas of the cities and towns have to disappear. Towns and cities lacking services have to go. If Mexican Americans have the political power of vote, it can happen and it will happen.

Chapter nine dealt with the issue of corruption. Unfortunately, the proximity of drug cartels in the immediate vicinity across the border affects, influences, and corrupts some people in the lower Rio Grande valley. The massive amount of money is a strong corruptive factor. Offers of massive amounts of money are as hard to resist here, as they are in Mexico. Again, massive amount of money is hard to resist everywhere as typically as in Washington DC. where of course it is a "legal" behavior. There is no corruption here.

Poverty can be traced as the root cause for many of our society's ills. Poverty is most frequently associated to gang activity and petty larceny, which can and often transitions into more serious crimes. It leads frequently to gangsterism, drug trafficking and murder. Poverty and the social ills brought about by poverty are common in struggling communities.

In the early days in this country the new immigrant groups were often the national groups involved in the illegal activity. Successive national groups: Irish, Italians, Jewish arrivals and others were often associated to illegal behavior. Mexican, Mexican Americans and other Hispanic groups are also involved in this undesirable activity. This problem affecting our national groups must end. This horrendous and violent behavior as seen in the portrayal of other national groups in computer games, television programs and the movies, while entertaining has to end. The negative stereotype of Hispanic Americans in the media has to end as well. The ability of parents to control what their children watch or do is increasingly difficult due to the many easy ways by which information is available. The social peer pressure is constant and unfortunately mostly negative. Parents must make an enormous effort to guide their children through this difficult problem in their lives These efforts must start as early as possible.

Fortunately, what makes parenting such a difficult job, if used appropriately, can make a world of difference. The internet is filled with all kinds of easily available information. Programs with positive educative value are easily identified. One can find actual primary school courses all the way up to university courses Parents should and must seek and identify high quality programs that can be an invaluable help in the children education. Hopefully with the initial parent's involvement the children can follow up these efforts and create a lifelong habit.

Poverty is not an excuse for bad behavior. Is up to the parents to make sure that their children know that. Is up to the parents to show the way. It is up to the parents to find a way to break out of poverty. Use of public support should be limited and only use in cases where and when other ways of helping the family are truly not available. The use of public support must be limited and never, never, never become routine. In this country of opportunity, as parents, it is your opportunity and responsibility to show the right way.

MEXICAN AMERICAN PRIDE
PRINCIPLE NUMBER 13

As a male I will treat all females with respect.

As a female I will expect and demand respect from males and other females and in return I will treat both with respect.

 IN THIS CHAPTER THE FOLLOWING POINTS ARE DISCUSSED:

1. Relations between men and women vary among racial and national groups.

2. Mexican and Mexican American men need to improve their behavior towards women.

3. Women's attitudes and societal roles are changing.

4. Teen parenthood is increasing. Parents need to be involved in guiding their girls and boys on sex education and their responsibilities.

5. Out-of-marriage birth rates are high and apparently increasing in all ages and racial groups.

6. The impact of teenage motherhood outside marriage has severe consequences for the single mother and the child.

7. The reasons for births outside marriage and their impact on teens are different from those for adults in the same situation.

8.   The key to improving relations between men and women successfully is self-respect between and among the sexes.

One of the most admirable qualities of American society is the respect given to women not only to women in the family but to all women. Respect for women and recognition of women as equal partners have grown over the years. This is in contrast to other societies where women are seen as property and subject to all types of abuse.

Among Mexican Americans as with Mexicans there is great respect to the point of veneration for women as mothers. In Mexico there is no greater holiday than Mother's Day. In the street things are different. Men tend to look at women they do not know as sexual objects. These women become the object of looks and at times of aggressive language. Of course, this can happen everywhere, particularly where men congregate and a woman on her own passes by. In crowded conditions such as in public transportation this aggressive and disrespectful behavior may at times involve unwanted touching. This behavior towards women is somewhat universal tendency but is more pronounced among the Latin men particularly the less well-educated men. Fortunately, this disrespect for women is becoming less frequent as women's status in the world and particularly in this country has risen.

Mexican Americans and Hispanics in general must improve their attitude towards females. As the twentieth-first century progresses females are becoming more and more successful in business, politics and education. In fact, many fields of study that previously were dominated by men have become populated by women. Medicine, law and even engineering have seen a greater number of females join their ranks to the point of outnumbering males in many cases. This occurs at all social and ethnic levels including in Mexican American dominated areas.

The rise of women in all fields has considerable societal consequences. Children of both sexes need parental guidance more than ever. It is essential that both males and females take more responsibility in procreation. For this to happen it is essential for parents to be more involved than ever.

For many years now, teen sexuality has been widely recognized and accepted. Because of many factors including social pressure it is very difficult for girls to avoid sexual activity. That is why parents, both fathers and mothers need to teach both young men and young women that bearing a child is the mutual responsibility of both sexes in the relationship. Usually girls and women end with the responsibility and the consequences, while the male at most is forced to pay child support. The life of the young mother is forever impacted while the young father is at liberty to lead a normal life. No longer can parents rely on school sex education programs. In many states sex education consists of emphasizing abstinence as if such behavior was always possible.

Many states governments are taking a moralistic stance as they are forced by religious influences to pretend that sexual problems do not exist. Federal and state governments nave banned essential services for women provided by charitable organizations with critical consequences. This governmental intrusion into women's rights is partly responsible for the dramatic increase in the number of births outside marriage occurring in our nation. Births out of wedlock are occurring in all age and all racial groups. In adults having a child without marrying is generally acceptable behavior. In teenagers, birth outside marriage is highly consequential for the young mother and her offspring. whose lives are forever negatively impacted. The problems women face are also by far more consequential for minorities, because the affluent can nearly always circumvent problems easier.

Females must respect themselves much better than they do. Such self-respect must be reinforced by parental teachings. Single motherhood in a teenager or young women is frequently a disaster waiting to happen. Children of single women are at a significant disadvantage when compared to their two parent peers. Teen motherhood is frequently either a sign of poor self-respect or ignorance of the consequences.

Single, out of wedlock motherhood happens in all ethnic groups and to women of all ages and has reached extreme numbers. It is more frequent in the less educated and unacceptably high in Hispanics. Repeat out of wedlock births are also frequent among Hispanic women. This situation must change for Mexican Americans to progress. Mexican American children must be given an opportunity for success in life. One essential step for this improvement is for Mexican and Mexican American men and women to respect each other much more than they do.

The birth rate in the United States have drop to historic low rates, even lower than in other low birth rate countries. The fall in birth rates has occurred in all ethnic groups but particularly among Hispanic women. The fertility rate was 1.76 in 2018 while the replacement rate to maintain a steady population is 2.1 births for woman. Statistics also point to a dramatic increase in births outside marriage in 2018 compared with the year 2000. There are reliable estimates indicating than the unmarried motherhood in Hispanic women is higher than in the non-Hispanic whites and lower than among blacks. Overall birth rates outside marriage are approximately 33% for non-Hispanic whites, 50% among Hispanic women and 75% among black women. The worst tragedy is that most Hispanic teen births are also single motherhood births, occurring while being high school students.

Among adults, births outside marriage have many reasons and often is a matter of choice. Career and professional pressures affect the choice to get married or not. Expectations of further economic improvement and for women pre-menopause considerations are all factors. Among adults and much less frequently in teens marriage may occur after an out of marriage birth.

Hispanic and particularly Mexican American men must make special effort to change disrespectful and aggressive behavior towards women. Latin-American women must respect each other and such groups as gangs and clicks must change to self-help and improvement groups. Women should respect themselves, avoid being willing victims of violence, sexual abuse and unwanted especially out of wedlock, pregnancies. Marital violence is abhorrent and sometimes ends tragically. Marital violence must not be tolerated and must be reported to authorities so protection can be found.

MEXICAN AMERICAN PRIDE
PRINCIPLE NUMBER 14

I will work steadily and as hard as I can
in my job or chosen profession and I will advance in it
as high as it is possible for me to advance.

 IN THIS CHAPTER WE WILL DISCUSS THE FOLLOWING:

1. Mexican Americans are very hard-working people but need to work in more productive occupations if progress as a group is to be attained.

2. When finding suitable employment, good behavioral practices are needed to succeed and advance in a chosen occupation or profession.

3. Education holds the key to success. Mexican American parents must support and encourage their children to study as hard as possible and qualify for college education.

4. Competition for college education has become extremely tough because of the arrival of Asian immigrants who are highly interested in their children to succeed. And succeed they do.

5. The educational success of Asian students offers for them significant employment advantage. While in contrast, their results put American students at a disadvantage.

6.   The success of Asian immigrants in the United States adds significant barriers to Mexican American education and Mexican American progress in general.

7.   In Texas high school graduates scoring in the highest 10th percentile are guaranteed the opportunity to attend Texas colleges. Similar opportunities in other states would result in better college educational opportunities for all American students.

8.   For Mexican American and Hispanic people to progress it is necessary to destroy educational and racial barriers. This will benefit the entire country by enabling all people to contribute to sustainable American greatness.

Mexican and Mexican- Americans are hardworking and dedicated people. Who has not seen migrant workers, laborers and camp and construction workers toil in such adverse conditions that less hardy people (most of us) could not endure? Some of us have seen poor Mexican laborers work their poor mountainous and dry land with the hope of growing some corn. That is an appalling sight.

No, there is no question Mexican-Americans can work as hard as anyone. The question is if this hard-working people should be working more efficiently and more productively. In order to do that, we need to elevate our aspirations. We need to find the right jobs and generally that requires exploring, planning, education and training. It also requires dedication and perseverance.

It cannot be emphasized enough, that education is the main key to obtaining a good job. Just as important is to perform well, once a good job is attained. Punctuality and enthusiasm for a well-done job are essential for advancement and success at work as they are in life. While performing well in your job, looking for ways to make the job more productive with ingenuity and initiative may be the key to advancement. Always look for better, more effective and more timely ways to perform the job at hand. Find improvements in associated processes. Always explore for opportunities to decrease cost, save time, increase productivity in your job or in jobs around you. As Hispanics we must develop and instill in our children the need to attain higher education and to develop excellent work habits, so they can excel and advance to the highest levels in the chosen field. As Americans it is essential that we perform at the highest level possible if our country is to remain as a leader in the twentieth-first century and beyond.

We as Mexican Americans have had difficulties in education attainment we must overcome. In the past, most Mexican Americans came to this country as poor, and often were illegal immigrants. Most of the Mexican American population were poorly educated and the only jobs available to them were menial type. Until ten to fifteen years ago the Mexican Americans practically avoided opportunities to obtain a college education. The high school dropout was in the high 70s or 80s. Since then the situation has changed for the better. Educational opportunities improve seemingly by the day. Education is not at the level it should be but there are hopeful signs. The hopes must be transformed into realities since there is and will be increasing competition for the good jobs and professional occupations.

The competition for the future success in the United States comes largely from recent Asian immigrants. Legal Asian immigration now is greater than legal Hispanic immigration. The Asian immigrants are well educated, being physicians, engineers and scientists for the most part. They have tremendous advantages over Americans. Education in most Asian countries as in Latin America is free or nearly free. The American student on the contrary is saddled with tremendous debt after university education and is in competition with a large number of applicants. The new educated Asian immigrants are demanding that their children obtain high grades in school. That dedication instilled by their parents makes Asian students able to compete with advantage for college entrance placement against non-Hispanic whites and of course against Hispanics who are still less well prepared to compete.

Recently, there are efforts by the United States government to change the immigration rules to prefer individuals with education and skills in preference to those who are not so qualified. That preference for better prepared immigrants, offers significant advantage to Asian students. They are products of societies who value education and discipline. In their home nations and here, in the United States children of Asian immigrants go to school to study. It seems that here, American students including Mexican-Americans go to school to play. Play they do, in all sports but prominently football. School systems throughout the nation, spend great amount of economic resources and time supporting sports that could best be dedicated to scholastic activities. The most tangible result of this dedication to sports is high school football. All television stations report high school scores to anxious and eager fans throughout the nation of "Friday Night Football." Scholastic football. is supposed to be an incubator for college and professional football players. If so, high school football is not working for Mexican Americans. Few Mexican American names are seen in College Football. Exceedingly few Mexican Americans play for the National Football League.

The educational disadvantage of Americans including Mexican Americans has severe consequences, even beyond the education area. The new well-prepared Asian immigrant population creates a large number of business and other enterprises. When generating new employment, they seem to prefer hard working immigrants similar to themselves who are generally happy with lower salaries. This behavior has two undesirable effects for American graduates. First, it lowers the opportunities of finding a good employment and second, it depresses the American graduate income, who all too often has to face overwhelming college education expense. The Asian population education success is even worrying the non-Hispanic whites to the point that they are more inclined to accept some degree of discrimination in college acceptance. This has become the subject of a challenge to Harvard University admission rules, where the Supreme Court ruled that discrimination as practiced by Harvard was acceptable and constitutional since Asians already occupied 40% of the available student places. Similar rates of Asian students exist in many other prestigious universities. In California Asian students dominate student populations throughout the state. In the state of Washington there was an attempt to restrict entrance of Asians to the State University. In this case the courts sided with the Asian students.

In Texas, Mexican American students graduating from Texas high schools have some help in accessing college education. All the students scoring in the upper 10% of their class are eligible to be admitted to a public Texas college. This provision by the Texas government evens the opportunities for college education for Mexican Americans significantly. It would be helpful if similar laws were enacted in all of the states of the union.

The picture for Mexican Americans who are in the lowest rungs of the educational ladder is extremely challenging. This situation must absolutely improve if we are going to succeed in improving the life of the neediest of us. The situation then is urgent. It has been pointed out that education costs in this country of ours is so high and so impossible for the average individual to afford that borders into the criminally expensive. Education costs must be lowered to the point that in-state education must be nearly free. Fortunately, lately some state and county colleges are offering significantly lower tuitions and many universities have decided to become tuition free.

We need not dwell on the fact that Hispanics rank the lowest of any other ethnic group in educational attainment, in participation at the highest level of government and in the financial world. We urgently need to change those dismal statistics. We as Hispanics need to do much better and we as Americans need to take responsibility to keep the country in the high standing it is. The European-American population is decreasing and the Hispanic-American population is increasing so that by 2150 and the foreseeable future, population projections indicate Hispanics will be the most numerous ethnic groups in the United States We need and must take up the challenge and succeed.

Groups that oppose the progress of Hispanics out of fear and racial concerns, are severely compromising the ability of the country to compete with others in the not distant and inexorable future. The Republican and Tea parties of today and the Democratic party of the recent past are in great part responsible for the lack of progress of the Hispanic population but

Hispanics and in particular Mexican Americans (we) are now the most culpable for remaining the most backward group.

The barriers for education and advancement are decreasing. It is possible for each of us to improve our educational and economic standing. It requires some ambition and imagination. Do not just do the job you are supposed to be doing. Look for opportunities to improve your standing in the job you have. Apply yourself without need for your supervisor or your boss to prod or ask you. Look for what can be done to make your work more effective. Is there any way that the job can be done faster or with less effort? Can there be an opportunity to coordinate two operations and make the job more effective? Is there any other job that could be more challenging to you and provide more personal satisfaction? Don't just stand still. There are opportunities everywhere.

MEXICAN AMERICAN PRIDE
PRINCIPLE NUMBER 15

I will take care of my health including maintaining healthy eating habits and avoid unhealthy habits such as smoking, excessive alcohol use and use of illegal drugs.

 IN THIS CHAPTER WE WILL DISCUSS THE FOLLOWING:

1. Mexican Americans as an ethnic group are predisposed to a group of diseases called: metabolic syndrome. This group of diseases include: diabetes, high blood pressure, obesity and increased blood lipids, including cholesterol.

2. This group of diseases when not treated leads to severe medical problems that include: non-healing ulcers, gangrene, foot, leg and entire extremity amputations, kidney failure, kidney failure treatments such as dialysis and kidney transplants (If lucky to find one), and blindness.

3. Mexican American dietary choices, cultural costumes and lack of exercise outside of work aggravates this group of diseases.

4. The Mexican and Tex-Mex restaurant industry bear significant culpability for the grave health consequences of serving huge caloric and fat laden menu servings. These large and unhealthy diets are also provided at home paralleling the restaurant offerings.

5. The restaurant industry could redeem itself by changing its philosophy and promoting healthy offerings in appropriately-sized servings.

6. Mexican American mothers and fathers and all Mexican American people must change their cultural behavior of qualifying fat babies and fat people as healthy. Fat babies and fat people are actually unhealthy people. They will suffer incredible health problems and painful deaths, if they do not slim down.

7. Slimming down is easy if people exercise and change dietary habits as recommended in this writing.

8. One of the most frequent cancers in Mexican Americans is cancer of the stomach. This cancer may in many instances related to reflux. Changing dietary habits very likely will decrease stomach cancer frequency among Mexican Americans. Cancer of the liver is also frequent among Hispanics and Mexican Americans. Cancer of the liver is associated with alcohol use and with liver inflammation (hepatitis). Cancer of the liver is often secondary to other cancers (breast, colon and rectum, lung, pancreas, lymphomas, etc.). Secondary cancer is called metastatic cancer and is highly frequent complication of other, ("primary") cancers. Other frequent organs site of metastatic cancer are lung and brain.

9. Cancer of the larynx, bronchus and lung is associated with smoking. The proportion of Latin Americans including Mexican Americans who smoke is high. Stopping tobacco use decreases frequency of lung cancer and other cancers frequently associated to smoking, including cancers of tongue, mouth, pancreas, kidney and bladder.

10. Breast and Cervix cancers Are more frequent and more lethal in Mexican American women than in non-Hispanic whites.

This is in great part because of delays in diagnosis and treatment. The closing of women's clinics such as Planned Parenthood will no doubt increase the incidence of these cancers in women. These closings were mandated by Republican administrations as a means of eliminate abortions. The consequence of these clinic closing, are increased unwanted pregnancies among low income teenagers and women. It will also result in increase in preventable diseases, including cervix and breast cancers and transmissible sexual diseases.

11. Cancer of the colon and rectum are less frequent in Mexican Americans than in other ethnic or racial groups. However, these cancers occur at a younger age in Hispanics. Awareness of this problem and vigilance is needed, for young Mexican Americans.

12. The frequency of cancer of the thyroid (mainly in women) and cancer of the prostate have been greatly exaggerated. Caution in proposed testing and treatment for these diagnoses must be exercised. The question to ask about the proposed diagnostic and treatment procedures in these cases is to ask: "Is this absolutely necessary?" Often the answer should be "No," we can wait.

13. Drug use is infrequent among Mexican Americans. "The war on drugs" has been an unnecessary wasteful and contra productive federal government effort to curb illegal drug trafficking and use. In the process of fighting this problem many Hispanic and black Americans have been arrested and jailed for minor drug use, while non-Hispanic white are exonerated of equivalent or more serious use.

14. A summary of recommendations helping health decisions for Mexican Americans and maybe most Americans regardless of race or ethnicity is presented at the end of this chapter.

Mexican and Mexican Americans are predisposed to metabolic disorders. Numerous studies have shown that rates of hypertension and obesity are high in comparison with other ethnic groups. Of particular concern is the marked predisposition to diabetes and its complications. This problematic metabolic predisposition is complicated by dietary choices. On the positive side Mexican Americans seem to have lower rates of heart attacks as a group.

Obesity is rampant among Mexican Americans. Along with high blood pressure and diabetes these conditions produce high rates of infirmity. These infirmities include renal failure and vascular circulatory problems that end up in lower extremity gangrene and amputations. Amputations are a daily occurrence in hospitals serving communities with higher Mexican Americans population.

Arterial vascular problems and insufficiency often begin to manifest as gangrenes of the toes, which after amputation are followed by foot amputation, then lower leg, stump, and mid-thigh amputations. At this point generally patients have well stablished renal failure that requires frequent dialysis and often, if available, renal transplants. Most patients also develop non-healing ulcers of the skin particularly in pressure areas such as hips. Some patients develop finger and hand gangrene that also require amputation. This course of real time events cannot continue. The cost in lives, the cost of disability and the economic loss is too great for the Mexican American population. For the entire society and the nation these costs are incredibility great to bear. The economic drag is crippling.

Predisposition to obesity may be genetic, but there are aggravating cultural circumstances. The first cultural factor is the equation of obesity in children with good health. If the baby or young child is heavy, obese with a round face, family and others will admire his appearance. They would say something like "your baby, (child), is a picture of health." Meaning that the baby is in an admirable good health. In reality if the nutritional and physical conditions do not change that child will have an unhealthy future. Childhood obesity is epidemic among Mexican American families.

The second circumstance resulting in obesity and metabolic syndrome development is lack of exercise. Lack of physical activity does not mean lack of activity linked to the profession or work but mere physical exercise such as walking, running, swimming, weight lifting etc. Fortunately, there is some evidence that these habits are changing. It is not uncommon now, to see organized physical activity events supported by local governments, community groups, health related institutions and enlightened commercial firms. These activities include runs for all age groups including "kids marathons." Also important are health information and health screening events that are supported by hospitals and businesses in the area, with the purpose of improving public health.

The most significant factor in development of the health and nutritional problems affecting Mexican Americans is their diet. In this area, great culpability is borne by the restaurant industry. Tex-Mex and Mexican restaurants are equally responsible. The problem is not so much the food types but the size of the servings. The size of the plates and the amount of food in the plate are much beyond the dietary needs of an individual. The amount of food served is generally good enough for two people or even enough for a family. At buffet type restaurants some people still go for "seconds" and "thirds" after they receive an initial large serving. The influence of restaurant behavior likely carries to home meals where large portions then also become the rule.

Mexican Americans need to change their behavior if they are to improve their health outlook. They have to do their utmost to avoid developing diabetes and its complications. If they do develop diabetes, they have to be faithful in its treatment. Diabetes sufferers need specific diets and appropriate treatments to keep blood glucose and hemoglobin A1C at therapeutic levels.

There are innumerable diets available and all of them require adherence to certain parameters to succeed in maintaining a healthy weight level. Most diets are tiresome and few succeed in eliciting enough dedication to be sustainable. The best dietary behavior is to eat a balance of all food elements including proteins, carbohydrates and lipids. Vegetables, fruits and nuts are indispensable in a healthy diet. Sufficient time must be dedicated when eating a meal (any meal). The mouthful of food eaten at a time needs to be of an appropriate, small size (for meat as an example not larger than half inch in diameter) and chewed multiple (at least twenty to thirty) times. This way of eating is healthy because chewing the food longer allows its flavor to be better appreciated. A second and most important advantage is that the stomach receives food that is more easily digested. In this way the stomach has to work less and there is almost no possibility of reflux and no need for antacid medication. Reflux can be entirely avoided if bed time occurs at a sufficient time (1 to 2 hours or longer) after the meal and if one is careful to lay down on the right side. Laying down on the right side after digestion helps empty the food into the intestine. A last but not to be dismissed advantage, is that if you chew your small portion of food multiple times you not only savor your food better, your stomach is free from reflux, but you also get tired of chewing. This way you eat less and control your weight without need of diets.

One of the most frequent cancers in Mexican Americans is cancer of the stomach. The incidence of gastric cancer in Mexican Americans is two to three times higher than among non-Hispanic whites. Gastric cancer occurs mostly in two portions of the stomach. The first portion of the stomach, next to and also affecting the esophagus is where most gastric cancers develop. This type of stomach cancer is very closely related to reflux. It makes sense that if food intake is properly managed as suggested in the above paragraph, the incidence of gastric cancer among Mexican Americans could decrease precipitously.

The incidence of unhealthy habits such as smoking and alcoholism is significantly higher among the Mexican American population. Smoking among Mexican Americans is moderate, lower than smoking among Puerto Rican Americans and Cuban Americans but higher than other Hispanic groups. The rate of smoking among Mexican American men is approximately 25% and 10% among women. It is preferable never to start smoking since it is addictive and for most people quitting is very difficult. The new epidemic particularly among the young is vaping. Vaping is proving to be a dangerous habit causing severe respiratory problems similar to chronic respiratory lung damage. Smoking is the cause of much disability and is the cause for most lung cancers. The occurrence of lung cancer among Mexican Americans is approximately one half as frequent as it is among non-Hispanic white men and women.

Alcoholism is high among Mexican and Mexican Americans. Alcoholism in combination with obesity and poor nutrition choices are partly responsible for liver cancer. Other factors such as viral hepatitis contribute to development of liver cirrhosis and cancer. Obesity and nutritional factors contribute to fatty liver disease and are factors in fatty related hepatitis. Liver cancer is one of the four cancers occurring more frequently in Mexican Americans than in non-Hispanic whites. Liver cancer frequency and mortality is double in Mexican Americans as compared to non-Hispanic whites.

Breast cancer in Hispanic and Mexican American women is less frequent than in non-Hispanic whites. However Mexican American women have lower rates of screening and use of early cancer detection methods. Because breast cancer is more advanced when Mexican American women are diagnosed and treated their mortality rate is higher. this more advanced breast cancer in Mexican American women at diagnosis accounts for the fact their mortality is higher than it is for non-Hispanic white females. Breast cancer is lower in foreign born women than in American born Hispanics

Cancer of the cervix in Mexican American women is more frequent and more lethal than in non-Hispanic whites. The same factors of lack of early detection and late initiation of treatment results in more advanced cases at diagnosis, more treatment failures and higher mortality. In the last fifteen to twenty years frequency and mortality of cervical cancer in Hispanic women actually decreased over half but is still much higher than in the non-Hispanic white women.

Cancer of the colon and rectum is less frequent among Hispanics than among non-Hispanic whites. This cancer also occurs at a younger age in Hispanics. Delays in diagnosis in Hispanics cause more severe disease at presentation for treatment and increased mortality. Decreased screening rates appear to be the most important determinant for this effect.

Cancer of the prostate in men and cancer of the thyroid in women are diagnosed very frequently but in both of these cases there is a great deal of overdiagnosis. In the case of cancer of the prostate there is oversampling by needle biopsies resulting in diagnosis of early inconsequential cases that will not progress to invasive cancers. In the case of thyroid cancer in women there is overdiagnosis of pathologic features and overdiagnosis of radiological changes. In both of these cancers there is significant difference and disparity between number of cancer diagnosis versus mortality figures. There is considerable discussion among medical circles about diagnostic and treatment criteria for these two cancers.

Illicit drug use by Mexican Americans is variable depending on immigration status, weather Mexican or United States born and in degree of acculturation. Undocumented Mexican migrants have negligible use of illicit drugs in contrast with alcohol use which is quite high. Use of illicit drugs by Mexican Americans born in Mexico is low. In Mexican Americans born in the United States illegal drug use is generally not high but depends of living location and association with groups such as gangs. The use of cannabis is much higher than for cocaine. The situation is in state of flux as more and more states legalize medical and recreational use of marihuana and derivatives. Use of synthetic and "fashion" illicit drugs appears more dangerous with overdoses and accidental deaths occurring frequently. Drug abuse in Mexican Americans is lower than in non-Hispanic whites. Use of illegal drugs and opioid pain killers by non-Hispanic whites is high enough that is affecting life expectancy statistics for the group.

The War on Drugs program of the United States is a complete failure that has resulted in greater rates of criminality, incarceration and pain especially for minorities. Illegal drug use and trafficking has caused too many deaths and disabilities. The drug wars have been particularly damaging in Mexico. There has been high member of deaths in drug cartel wars between drug cartel people and the opposing military. Deaths have been numerous among innocent bystanders. There is also a great increase in criminality among people and groups who take advantage of the fear created drug trafficking.

There is a basic error in treating drug abuse. Drug abuse should be treated as an addiction that calls for treatment rather than as a crime that needs to be punished. Instead of burning and destroying confiscated drugs, they should be stockpiled and used for treatment of the addicted. There are better options to combat drug traffic such as cocaine. Mexico should overcome the fear of the United States military and the United States should give more credit to the Mexican government and their armed forces. Contrary to the United States the Mexican military are used only to maintain the internal peace and to help in cases of disasters and other sizeable internal needs. There should be honest discussions between United States and Mexico to negotiate a strategic combined military group to intercept the marine illicit drug transport. A combined naval base could be located in the Pacific coast near the border with Guatemala. Similar but simpler treaty between United States and Colombia gave access to military American forces in the country and appears successful in ameliorating the worse effects of drug traffic there.

As a way of summation in the health area for Mexican American and Hispanic the following facts appear to be pertinent:

1. Hispanics are a varied ethnic group and are not racially homogeneous. Health and cultural differences affect variability of all findings between Hispanic groups. Therefore, when we say Hispanics it may or may not apply to Mexican Americans and when we say Mexican Americans may or may not to apply to other Hispanics.

2. Mexican Americans are predisposed to metabolic disorders which include: Obesity, hypertension and diabetes and their complications.

3. Mexican Americans need to moderate their diet, change their eating behavior and their cultural perception of obesity to avoid the ravages of metabolic disorders. Otherwise they are faced with enduring group of disabling maladies such as dia-

betes, arterial vascular disorders, renal failure, amputations and blindness.

4. Mexican Americans need to develop the habit of physical exercise in any modality. They must take advantage of community walking or running events and community health screening programs.

5. Mexican Americans should avoid restaurants that serve excessive meal portions and if they cannot, then share meals or ask for smaller servings instead. Taking home some of the food is a good alternative It would be better to patronize restaurants that serve smaller, tastier and satisfying meals. In any case they must take meals in small portions, chew food multiple times and end eating when satisfied instead of eating everything in the plate.

6. Weight loss diets have little success rate and eventually fail at the end. A moderate balanced intake of all nutrients eaten slowly and carefully is the best solution to nutrition.

7. Smoking is still common in Mexican Americans but it is gradually decreasing. Smoking causes chronic lung disease and lung cancer among other diseases. Quitting smoking is difficult for all but a few people but it is a worthwhile thing to do because it decreases the likelihood of developing a serious illness.

8. Stomach cancer is much higher among Mexican Americans compared with non-Hispanic whites and any other ethnic or racial group. Eating as slowly and carefully as suggested may result in near total and permanent relief of reflux and a highly significant reduction in frequency of gastric cancer.

9. Liver cancer is nearly twice as frequent in Mexican Americans compared to non-Hispanic whites. Reduction in alcohol in-

take, reduction in obesity and better nutritional selection could help reduce liver cancer incidence.

10. Breast cancer is less frequent in Mexican American women but delays in diagnosis cause larger breast cancers at presentation for surgery and increased mortality. Hispanic women should have mammography as recommended, to have an earlier diagnosis and better treatment options. If this is done, breast cancer should have frequent cures and lower mortality. Currently that is not the case unfortunately. Breast cancer is the most frequent cancer in women and has the highest mortality. Mortality could be greatly reduced if Hispanic women would have testing done as recommended. Testing is often avoided because of economic considerations but hospital and radiology services often offer discounted rates at special events.

11. Cancer of the colon and rectum is less frequent in Mexican Americans than in non-Hispanic whites but delays in diagnosis frequently results in larger incurable cancers and unnecessary high mortality. Men and women must have colonoscopies as recommended. Actually, colonoscopy should by started earlier because in Hispanics colorectal cancer occurs at an earlier age. Colorectal cancer is the second most frequent cause of death in Hispanic men and women.

12. Cancer of the prostate is by far the most frequent cancer diagnosis in men and thyroid cancer is the second most frequent cancer diagnosis in women. These two cancers are frequently over diagnosed and also overtreated. In the case of prostatic cancer numerous unnecessary needle biopsies are taken with the intension of not missing the smallest prostate lesion. This results in diagnosing minimal lesions that may never progress to real cancer. Many patients with this diagnosis may die with prostate cancer but not because of it. Prostate cancer biopsies

should not be undertaken without the benefit of a good rectal exam where the cancer can easily be felt as an indurated area. Cancer of the thyroid is too frequently over diagnosed in women. Radiologic findings of nodules are frequently the spark that initiates biopsies. The criteria for biopsy diagnosis of thyroid cancer are currently under review. Mortality because of thyroid cancer is almost unheard of. Mortality caused by prostatic cancer is low and disproportional with the number of diagnosed cases. Advanced prostatic cancer can metastasize extensively.

13. Illegal drug abuse is less frequent in Hispanics than in other racial or ethnic groups It is infrequent in Mexican Americans born in Mexico and more frequent in United States born Mexican Americans. It is nearly absent in undocumented immigrants. Illegal drug use is nevertheless a most frequent cause for Hispanic incarceration.

14. To combat drug trafficking and drug use a new approach is needed. The current war on drugs and similar approaches are of no use and frequently contra productive.

MEXICAN AMERICAN PRIDE
PRINCIPLE NUMBER 16

 IN THIS CHAPTER WE DISCUSS THE FOLLOWING:

1. The story of the trapped bugs and its application to Mexican American progress and the suffering of low skill workers.

2. The need for successful Mexican Americans to support farmworkers and unskilled workers in their struggles to have a better life.

3. The need to recognize as highly valuable the work these workers perform and afford them the respect they deserve.

4. The necessity to help these workers to succeed in their struggles because it is essential for all Americans to lift the esteem of these workers. For European Americans these workers are the image representative of what all Mexican Americans are. If their living conditions and appreciation of their work do not improve, all Mexican Americans will be treated with disrespect and consider not worthy of American citizenship. Mexican Americans will be considered not real Americans." Yes, they are Americans, but not really... real Americans."

5. The jobs that farmworkers and non-skilled workers do cannot be abandoned because no other group is willing to do it. These workers should be provided the opportunity to acquire skills that enable them to transition to more satisfactory occupations. At the very least, their children should have these opportunities.

6. Mexican American business owners must provide clean, pleasant facilities for their customers. They must strive to give the best service possible at the most economical yet competitive price possible

7. Mexican American and Hispanic professionals must educate their communities providing advice on how to live healthier, more productive and more satisfying lifestyles.

8. Mexican American business owners and entrepreneurs should move into more advanced fields that provide occupations related to STEM and AI (artificial intelligence) fields.

9. Lastly, Mexican American and Hispanic business owners must treat their employees fairly and with respect.

I heard a story in my younger years that goes like this: There was once a large concave glass bowl in which there were a mix of small bugs straining to get out by climbing the slippery glass walls. There was a mixture of bugs. There were Jewish bugs, Arab bugs, Chinese bugs, American bugs and Mexican bugs. The struggling bugs would get help from their own nationality bugs and eventually they reached the bowl rim and be free. Every nationality bug would get out. Every bug that is, except the Mexican bugs. Because every time that a Mexican bug would reach the bowl rim another Mexican bug standing by the bowl rim would kick the Mexican bug back into the bowl bottom.

This story has probably been said many times by many people with the bug nationalities changed. In Mexico many people think that the story has strong hints of truth in it seeing as how Mexicans and, in this case,

Mexican Americans and other Latins struggle to succeed. In any case I hope that we all believe what is patently true. As long as Mexicans and Mexican Americans stand on the bottom rung of the success ladder all of us will be judged incapable, indolent and backward. Just read what Tom Brokaw said about Mexican Americans and the future of the country. And don't kid yourself that is what most Americans worry about.

It is obvious then, that all of us Mexican Americans have to help our brothers living at the bottom of the economy, out into the world of success. As long as there are undocumented Mexican immigrants or simply undocumented immigrants crossing the southern border: and as long as Mexican Americans work in most menial jobs, most European Americans will not recognize our contributions to the American success story.

As we have said in past chapters it is extremely important to recognize as the work that our Mexican and Mexican American brothers and sisters perform in agriculture, in construction, in the service of hospitality industry as highly valuable. Equally important is their work helping families in the care of the home, as custodians and in a myriad of occupations that most people consider menial. Without the labor this group performs the country would literally not function. All of us, Mexican, Mexican Americans and Hispanic must support these workers in their struggle for better working conditions, better compensation, and for better treatment. The value of their work must be acknowledged by all Americans.

There is no question these occupations are necessary and vital for the country to succeed, progress and even to function. It is just as necessary for Mexican Americans and Hispanics to explore ways to allow and facilitate the growth of these workers so they can evolve into positions in technical, business and professional fields. We must make sure that these workers and their families, particularly their children, have the educational and other means of support to make this possible. Technical and vocational schools, community colleges and university education must all be made possible and accessible. Entrepreneurism must be stimulated. In other words, all avenues for progress must be accessible. That is what has made America great and that has to be what we, Mexican Americans and Hispanic must do. This is vital not only for our people, it is vital for our country. We must join the other better incorporated national groups. We can no longer be the "less American" group. In fact, we are essential to our country's future. We cannot let racist, nationalistic, supremacist attitudes of the effete, get us down. Most Americans, "the good Americans" should and will support our efforts.

Mexican Americans have a diversity of businesses but frequently seem to be focused on the food industry, Mexican and Tex-Mex restaurants, bakeries, meat markets and Mexican food supermarkets are frequently run by Mexican Americans. They run, however all kinds of small businesses in nearly all areas of human endeavor too numerous to mention. It is important that all of us Mexican Americans and Hispanics support and patronize these businesses. It is just as important that Mexican American and Hispanic businessmen and businesswomen strive to have attractive clean operations providing attentive, honest and pleasant service to clients. It is extremely important for clients to feel that they have been treated well and given the best value for the services or goods provided.

Professional activities of Mexican Americans and Hispanics deserve special attention. It is unfortunate that at this time the Mexican American population is one of the poorest in the country and that it is inadequately served by medical and health services. Much can be done by Mexican Americans to improve their own health as discussed in Chapter 15. Genetic predisposition to metabolic disorders: hypertension, obesity and diabetes are only made worse by dietary choices. If the issues dealt with in Chapter15 can be resolved, Mexican Americans could look forward to the prospect of good health. Improving the health of Mexican Americans requires the involvement of the entire community. One of the primary responsibilities resides within the medical community. Obstetricians and midwives should talk to prospective mothers about healthy upbringing of the newborn. Pediatricians should educate the mother about healthy weight and good nutrition. Nurses should educate themselves on the issues and transmit the knowledge to families. Family doctors, internists and other primary care practitioners have a distinctive opportunity to approach the subject while treating the patient. All of these individuals must take the responsibility to educate, and in that way prevent the serious health problems that affect our Mexican American community. These health problems should be prevented. Treatment without education is nearly certain to be insufficient to prevent negative outcomes: infirmity disability and death.

The nursing profession has a great future. Mexican American women have a natural predisposition to perform well in this profession. Mexican American men likely do as well. The nursing profession is likely to do well in the era of artificial intelligence that will probably replace many other jobs. Nursing school opportunities are open to Mexican Americans and high school students seem to have taken notice and are expressing great interest in them. We, the Mexican American community desperately needs Mexican American physicians. The number of Mexican American doctors is woefully inadequate in relation to the number and the needs of the Mexican American population in the country. Recent opening of new medical schools with high percentage of Mexican American and Latin students will help but will not be enough to satisfy the needs.

Mexican Americans and Hispanics need to be more involved in the science, technology, engineering and mathematics (STEM) fields. Fortunately, interest in education is flourishing among Mexican American students and there seems to be an interesting future in this area of learning ad practice. We shall soon see.

Because of the nature of the work Mexican Americans perform, they are often abused particularly if they are undocumented. As a Mexican American or Hispanic employer, you must treat your employees fairly. You should pay more than the minimum federal wage guidelines stipulate which is not sufficient to even cover living expenses. You must pay overtime. Pay fair wages on time.

Violations of these rules are frequent and unfortunately Mexican and Mexican American employers are also guilty of breaking them. These violations should be reported to the employment authorities. Reporting individuals should be treated as whistleblowers with the proper rules applied when authorities take up the case.

MEXICAN AMERICAN PRIDE
PRINCIPLE NUMBER 17

I will not use services of businesses or enterprises that discriminate against Mexican Americans, Hispanics, minorities and other national or racial groups.

 IN THIS CHAPTER WE WILL BE DISCUSSING THE FOLLOWING:

1. Discrimination against minorities including Hispanics and Mexican Americans has always been present in the United States. The worst years seem to be behind, however it has not disappeared. The truth is that we, Mexican Americans are partially responsible for this behavior because we have erected barriers that makes us comfortable in our culture and heritage. It is time that we come out of the comfort zone and become active citizens of the United States. It is time that we become true, proud Americans.

2. Let us prove racist, supremacist, erratic, above the law, sexually abusive Trump that he is wrong about us. We, Mexican American and Hispanics are hardworking, responsible, loyal and good members of American society.

3. Historically the anti-Mexican American racism was most prevalent, violent and criminal in the Southwestern States. Some of that racism is still prevalent and cruel in Texas and Arizona. As Mexican Americans and immigrants have moved

into the southern states, the discriminatory environment has moved with them.

4. Along with discriminatory treatment, efforts to disenfranchise and to minimize the power of the Mexican American vote in Texas, has gained impetus under the majority Republican state government.

5. Historically both the Democratic and Republican parties have treated Mexican Americans and Hispanics in a racist manner. The Anglo members likely remain the same, but with the advent of the Civil Rights Act of 1964 they changed allegiances turning Democrats into Republicans. Therefore, we have to make certain to vote for the party more likely to help us in the progress we seek.

6. At this time, we Mexican Americans must favor the Democratic Party with our vote, but we must also make certain that our needs are taken care of. We know that some Mexican Americans whether because of assimilation, economic reasons or otherwise, vote Republican. However, it is extremely important that they help other Mexican Americans in their effort to improve themselves and improve perception of all Mexican Americans.

7. The increase in Hispanic population which is the most numerous in the country after non-Hispanic whites makes their purchasing power important key in ending most discriminatory practices. This end, provided that the purchasing power is synchronous with voting power. The obvious thing is then to become United States citizens and use those most important rights, registering to vote and voting. We Hispanics and Mexican Americans can be the masters of our destiny. In that way we can become valuable citizens of the United States of America.

8. Few anti-Mexican American, anti-Hispanic and anti-immigrant organizations are more powerful than Fox News except maybe, the Republican Party itself. It is important to recognize and respect the power of this organization. It is important to make it as ineffective as possible but that would be hard, nearly impossible. Trump and Fox News are the enemy. Recognize and understand both.

9. The absence of Hispanics and Mexican Americans in the American television and movie industry while the opposite happens in the Hispanic channels is creating of a sort of quasi-apartheid. This, somehow, we need to avoid. The black American experience must be our guide.

Mexican Americans need to be constantly vigilant in identifying open or masked threats against minorities. Mexicans, Mexican Americans and people of Mexican descent. are the favorite group to attack in this country. Much of the attack against them is related to illegal immigration. Even than most immigrants are refugees from the northern triangle of Central America the brunt of the attacks seem centered on Mexico and Mexican Americans.

In his presidential campaign, Donald Trump received a great boost to his candidacy through his vilification of Mexicans, thereby exacerbating attacks on Mexican Americans by doing so. His statement of Mexicans being criminals coming illegally across an open border, aroused racism among white supremacists who fear being outnumbered in this country.

Historically, racism has been constant in the southwest particularly in Texas, Arizona and sporadically in New Mexico, Colorado, and California. In Texas the anti-Mexican feeling is exacerbated by statements and actions of Governor Abbot and by his criminally indicted Attorney General Ken Paxton supported by the Republican majority in the upper and lower chamber. Passage of SB4 which bans so-called "Sanctuary cities." This law forces local officials to act as immigration agents and ask anyone they stop or arrest as to their immigration status. This, of course, mainly targets Mexican Americans and Hispanics. Attempts at disenfranchising of individuals of Hispanic surname, and Gerrymandering to decrease and dilute Mexican American voting power are further evidence of discrimination These actions are the tip of the iceberg in Texas ever-present fear and disdain of Texans for the Mexican American population. Texas stands prominently for its anti-Dreamer stance and the suit that was echoed by many of the other Republican state governors. Texas was also the center against President Obama's attempt to protect parents of Dreamers.

Arizona has a long history of anti-Mexican attitudes dating from the Mexican American war peace treaty signing. The Anti Mexican American discrimination in Arizona was and still is as pronounced and, in some ways, worse than in Texas. All types of abuse of Mexican Americans have been documented in Arizona. Histories of indiscriminate murder and Lynching in Arizona abound. Coper mine strikes early in the twentieth century resulted in illegal deportation of Mexican Americans. The history of discrimination of Mexican Americans in Arizona has not abated and was freshly renewed with anti-immigrant laws that have recently past and partially upheld by the Supreme Court of the nation. Sheriff Arpaio re-elections occur despite being indicted for anti-Mexican and anti-Hispanic profiling and treatment of the jail prisoners. His anti-Mexican and anti-Hispanic actions were rewarded by Trump, who pardoned him.

Obviously, the Republican Party in Arizona is shamelessly an anti-Mexican American, anti-Hispanic and anti-immigrant organization, which should be rejected and condemned by all Hispanics. The Republicans were supported in past elections by groups of Mexican Americans who refused to recognize their party's anti-Mexican American attitude and preferred to support a group that will keep their taxes low and discourage social programs to help the poor. Some supporters of the Republican Party do so because they are opposed to abortion and to acceptance of the LGBTQ gendered population. Mexican Americans at this time in our History must support the Democratic Party. We should be careful and base our support on the support that Mexican American people get in return. We must stop the lip support we usually receive from officials we helped elect. We must settle only for meaningful favorable action that addresses our needs. We

MUST remember that the Republican Party of the present was the Democratic Party of the past, when Mexicans along with negroes and dogs were not welcomed in many public places.

Most of the southwestern states were governed by Democrats when massive number of Mexican and Mexican Americans, 60% of them American citizens were summarily thrown out of their homes and deported to Mexico. Many more people were scared into leaving the country instead of facing deportation. The reason they were deported was the scarcity of jobs during the depression years. Jobs it was said, were only for REAL Americans, white European-Americans. Presently there is a real possibility in near future of massive job losses due to the rise of Artificial Intelligence ([AI). AI will replace human manual and intellectual human labor with automatic and robotic procedures. that will make intelligent human labor unnecessary. Let us hope that history of deportations because of job losses does not repeat itself. Obviously, we Mexican Americans have to become "REAL Americans" by then. We must make the Mexican American Pride dream a reality. There is no other way, it is inexorably the way

In Texas and Arizona, the dominant Republican Party has been particularly anti-Mexican American. However, these two states could easily turn Democratic if Mexican Americans would register and vote.

There are now few openly anti-Mexican and anti-Mexican American institutions or businesses. Perhaps the reason why, is that there are over sixty million Mexican-Americans and people of some Mexican and Hispanic descent in the United States. The economic power of these sixty million people is possibly a deterrent to open anti-Hispanic attitudes. The opposite, pro-Hispanic and pro-Mexican American attitude could become possible if the power of the vote would be commensurate with the economic power of Hispanic people. This is a remainder to Mexican Americans that they must register and vote as Cuban Americans Jewish Americans, Indian-Americans, Chinese Americans and other minorities do. Like those minorities, we have veiled detractors whom we must unmask, neutralize and defeat. We must always be on guard, be particularly vigilant of social media conversations. We must avoid another El Paso.

The only openly Anti-Mexican American and anti-immigrant business is Fox News which supports Trump in his anti-Mexican anti- immigrant diatribe. Some Fox News people are particularly rabid in their pro-Trump. pro-border wall, anti-immigrant talk, others are more tolerable and even enjoyable. One would like to invoke the power of the Hispanic economic power to silence Fox News's anti-Mexican American attitude by asking the pro-Mexican American businesses to stop advertising on their channel. However, dissent and freedom of the press are too important to be suppressed. Interestingly, other stations of the Fox Network do not promote the same causes as Fox News.

Throughout the country there are now a few anti-Hispanic and anti-immigrant conservative radio hosts. The same can be said for newspaper writers and publishers. All of these sources of negative information about Hispanics and Mexican Americans must be identified for what they are, avoided and ignored.

The best way to discredit these negative information sources is to improve the Mexican American and Hispanic community. The best way to advance Mexican American and Hispanics, attaining recognition as valuable citizens in American society is for us all to follow the steps outlined in *Mexican American Pride* The country overall will be better off for this effort.

One bothersome fact is the absence of significant numbers of Mexican American and Hispanic people on television, in the movie industry and involved in television programing. There is to be sure a significant presence of Hispanic people on the Hispanic networks, but we must be careful not to create an apartheid type of attitude and behavior. We have to find a way to develop a significant presence on the English language television and in the movie industries. Let us try to follow the example of African Americans who not long ago had limited presence in the media and who now are seen everywhere both in black and biracial situations.

MEXICAN AMERICAN PRIDE
PRINCIPLE NUMBER 18

I will patronize and support businesses and enterprises that support Mexican American and Hispanic causes.

 IN THIS CHAPTER THE FOLLOWING IS DISCUSSED:

1. There are many Mexican American and Hispanic organizations working to present and advance solutions to issues affecting the Latino and Hispanic community. These organizations may be sources of help to an individual or a group. In turn those institutions need and deserve moral and economic support from all Hispanics and Latinos.

2. Most of the Hispanic organizations participate in a program called: Hispanic Association on Corporate Responsibility. (HACR) its ultimate objective is to modify corporate behavior to increase the number of Hispanic employees, Hispanic suppliers and board members in corporate management. It makes possible for Hispanics to fill positions in corporate structures.

3. Brief descriptions of the most important Mexican American and Hispanic advocating organizations follow. The area or areas of involvement on behalf of Hispanics is described. Their successes and failures are discussed. Further ways that the different associations could help are also discussed.

4. There is substantial optimism that Mexican American, Hispanic and Latino communities are at the beginning of a renaissance in which they take their place in the American success story and achieve the dream.

There are many large organizations in this country that support and promote Mexican American and Hispanic causes and institutions. There are advocacy organizations that work against discrimination, that provide for legal help and work for favorable public policy changes Many organizations concern themselves with changes to immigration policies and helping DREAMERs. Still others help with educational opportunities, with work situations and improving housing, environmental conditions and public services. All of these organizations deserve support of Mexican Americans and Hispanics.

Most of the Hispanic and Mexican American organizations participate in a study group called Hispanic Association on Corporate Responsibility (HACR). This group investigates and reports the degree to which members of HACR hire Hispanic employees, in what proportion they use Hispanic suppliers and to what degree they use Hispanics in their corporate boards. They also catalog the company involvement in philanthropic activities. Corporate responsibility is a relatively new concept that involves companies having or developing plans to be socially responsible Among these responsibilities or values is workforce diversity. They have had some success in increasing the number of Hispanics employees, suppliers and to some degree the number of board members

New college graduates and any Hispanic individual would be well advised to contact any of the sponsoring organizations to find out about employment opportunities among the participating corporate members. The sponsoring organizations should work on establishing lists of potential available employees available to submit to the HACR members. They could also have lists of Hispanic suppliers. In previous chapter (Chapter 1) we have discussed the plight of the farmworker. We have also said that one of the ways to seek relief for these workers, is with the involvement of grocers and other buyers of agricultural and farm products. HACR is a possible mechanism to convert the concept into reality

One of the largest, and the first and continuously functioning Hispanic organization is the League of United Latin American Citizens (LULAC). It was established in 1927 in Texas mostly by veterans returning from World War I. The group was concerned with the status of Mexican Americans. The issues then, were not much different from the issues that persist to the day.in many Mexican Americans communities. In the one hundred years since, many of those issues have been ameliorated but the distance to success is still considerable. In many ways the problem is not because of them (The Anglos) who we blamed before and still do, to some extent. The problem is not Trump and the Republicans; the problem is us. The means to get ahead, are ours. We need to get going. We live in the country of opportunity and we are uncaring, lazy of intellect, morose and weak. We are conformist, easily give up and jealous of those who succeed. We need to become active American citizens, we must support and impulse our children to success, maintain and improve our physical and mental health. There is so much we need to do but we can do it. Remember: "yes, we can"

LULAC was organized to combat discrimination which in those days was of the worst kind, Apartheid-like. LULAC was also organized to promote and advance economic conditions, education, housing and health, civil rights and political involvement. Because LULAC membership only accepted U.S. citizens it was against further Latin immigration particularly because the unskilled character of the new immigrants, their working for very low wages, lowering their own earnings. LULAC won many and significant battles in their quest for Hispanic equality. For instance, LULAC won legal battles in education that reinforced the Supreme Court decision of Brown VS. Board of education of Topeka,347 U.S.483 and the previous civil rights legislation. The organization also won a suit to allow Hispanics to serve in juries Currently LULAC also provides direct student help in the form of grants and fellowships and helps in Hispanic employment.

The American GI Forum (AGIF) was established in 1948 to address issues related to Mexican American veterans. Initially it was concerned with medical services for veterans that were denied to Mexican American veterans. The AGIF soon pursued other Mexican American veteran issues including educational issues, Mexican American civil rights, voting rights and jury selection. The AGIF has numerous chapters all over the nation but particularly in Texas. The AGIF should have a full plate of issues. The treatment of veterans in this country is shameful. The Veterans Hospitals and clinics for veterans are shameful, `Doctors working for veteran's clinics and hospitals complain to the fact that the system is riddled with physicians who fake working and attending veterans while having a good lazy time putting the hours and leaving the work to a few doctors who really care. Despite all the promises, services for veterans are a national shame.

In addition to poor medical services there are, everywhere in the country, the homeless veterans, the veterans suffering from post-traumatic shock syndrome. A specially vexing situation is that of veterans, who having served honorably in the United States forces are deported to Mexico for minor violations often induced by their psychologic and psychiatric problems. Some of the deported veterans are Mexican American citizens. Others are Mexican nationals who had been promised American citizenship after serving but forgot or neglected to apply. Veteran Services, mut remediate this injustice and the GI Forum must make a priority to do something about all of these issues. The United States should do something real to treat veterans the way they deserve. A "thank you for your services" greeting is not enough. Veterans hospitals associated to Universities and Medical schools seem to perform better. Veterans clinics must have rigid rules and standards for physicians who serve there. If those measures do not work, veterans must have clear and free access to public hospitals and public practitioners.

Unidos US, formerly LA RAZA changed its name Unidos US to be more inclusive but, in the process, lost the connotation of our common, European, Latin-American bond. Unidos US has a large number of affiliates throughout the country, and has a large number of sponsoring businesses. Unidos US was founded in 1968. Unidos US and is the largest Hispanic organization dedicated to advocacy for the Latino community. Unidos US dedicates its efforts in all sectors of interest to the advancement of the Mexican American and Hispanic peoples in this country. The association seeks political change and public policies that favor progressive improvements in the economic, educational and social status of Hispanics. It concerns itself with improvements to housing, community development, and labor issues including job training. Unidos US advocates for DACA recipients, helps orient students in college readiness and STEM careers; Science, Technology, Engineering and Mathematics. The association is active in promotion of adult education and voter registration. With all of these activities Unidos US seeks to improve the standing of the Latino population in the United States.

The great number of Unidos Us advisors, affiliates and sponsors read like a Who is Who in America. It would be of great help to Mexican Americans and Hispanics if these businesses would lend a hand for employment of the individual. For that purpose, it may be worth to try to contact Unidos US. At the Washington DC headquarters or in the regional offices in Chicago, Los Angeles, Miami, New York, Phoenix or San Antonio or perhaps any of the affiliates through the United States. Alternatively contact any of the sponsor directly. Unidos Us is also a member sponsor of The Hispanic Association on Corporate Responsibility The members of this group as explained before are committed to increase the number of Hispanic Employees, Hispanic suppliers, to increase the number of Hispanics sitting in their corporate boards and to increase philanthropic activities directed toward Hispanic sources. These corporations can and should be used as resources for employment opportunities and as possible clients for Mexican American and Hispanic businesses.

MALDEF (Mexican American Legal Defense and Educational Fund) Provides legal aid help, and advocates for changing laws that make educational opportunities fairer. MALDEF also won a suit against re-districting in Texas and another suit against the state of Arizona. MALDEF has been instrumental in educational reforms favoring Hispanics in an effort to make the education field fairer and balanced among the racial divide.

MALDEF also has initiated legislation to make elections more transparent avoiding unfair and discriminative actions against Hispanics. The organization has also worked for the fair treatment of immigrants. MALDEF activities and support would be of great help in securing passage of a` bill favoring implementation of a Blue Card. The Blue Card would make legal and regularize the residence and working rights of farmworkers and other low wage workers.

La Union del pueblo Entero (LUPE} founded by Cesar Chavez and Dolores Huerta in 1989 to help small Texas communities in the Lower Rio Grande Valley. The association concerns itself with issues related to colonia living, fair treatment of immigrant workers and access to medical services and education. Another important issue concerns colonia infrastructure improvement, including that of water quality, sewers, drainage, lighting, and street paving. Dealing with floods is a major problem in many communities. The needs of the colonias inhabitants are identified during colonia meetings and solutions are proposed. Lupe's civic activities include working for voting rights, voter registration and census participation. Housing improvement is sorely needed in many colonias. Texas colonias have a voice that seems to help their communities. There are also established colonias in New Mexico, Arizona and California. Housing in colonias could be easily improved using a mechanism employed by Habitat for Humanity. This would involve providing low cost repayable loans and making use of the so-called "sweat equity" whereby the beneficiaries perform the work needed for building and remodeling.

The Congressional Hispanic Caucus and the Congressional Hispanic Conference are groups that could help our legislative agenda. Unfortunately, they are divided by their political affiliation along Democrat and Republican Party lines. Ideally, they would work together to help, even lead in advancing Hispanic causes. Instead they get bogged down and lost in squabbles of political nature. We should, actually expect that these elected officials behave as they promised and do something for us, Hispanics who are in so much need of true political leaders. In a previous chapter we have discussed the need for a third party. A mediator party that would look after the people's needs and have mentioned that a caucus of Hispanic legislators looking after the needs of Hispanics, could be an intermediate step. We Hispanics need for this Caucus to function much better. We also need the Hispanic organizations discussed in this chapter to amply communicate their needs and ideas to the Caucus.

The United States Hispanic Chamber of Commerce (USHCC) helps businesses to succeed by providing guidance, connections and opportunities for growth. The USHCC is a good source when starting or growing a business, looking for partners, funding etc. The Chamber is also involved in educational issues such as impulse to STEM education and leadership training. Other issues are women empowerment and women businesses and leadership. The Chamber supports and stimulates small and minority business development There are over two hundred Hispanic chambers of commerce throughout the United States.

The list of members, donors, associates and affiliates for LULAC, Unidos US, the Hispanic Chamber of Commerce and other Hispanic organizations is comprehensive. It is a listing of American financial, industrial, commercial, communications and hospitality world etc. In other words, the cooperating organizations includes most of the shakers and movers in the country. The number of affiliates, donors and advisors participating in Unidos US is impressive. These organizations understand the economic power and the potential political power of over sixty million Mexican Americans and Hispanics. We need to unleash that potential and make it real. We need to venture out and emerge into a dynamic world, vital to America. Our Mexican American and Hispanic cultural roots are strong and combined with the American dynamism can lead to a near magical, great and winning combination.

With the help of these organizations, some imagination and gentle pressure, we can find the solution to our most pressing problems. We could help our farmworkers to obtain a better deal from their employers and help those without documents obtain the proposed Blue Card that would free them from the threats they confront daily. We could also accomplish our educational, economical, health and political objectives. We can and we must find the way to do our part for the country's continuing prosperity and progress. The future is ours for the taking.

MEXICAN AMERICAN PRIDE
PRINCIPLE NUMBER 19

Forget the Alamo as a symbol of Anglo supremacy
and source of discriminatory practices against Mexican
Americans and Mexican American heritage.

 In this chapter the following is discussed:

1. The historical background to Texas independence from Mexico.

2. Mexico inability to control and hold onto the Spanish inheritance of New Spain.

3. Mexico's solution for controlling and populating Texas was to invite Europeans and Americans to colonize Texas.

4. Mexico's conditions for migration to Texas were loyalty to Mexico, learning Spanish, converting to Catholicism and renunciation of slavery. With few exceptions those conditions were not met and therefore the migration was illegal.

5. The primary reason for the Texas rebellion was the change in Mexico from the Federal constitution of 1824 to a centrist one. The 1824 constitution was patterned after the United States Constitution. The Federal constitution guaranteed States rights, while the Central constitution abolished States rights and converted states into departments ruled from Mexico City.

6. Tejanos (Mexican Texans) as well as American Texans supported the rebellion. The rebellion against the change in the constitution also occurred in many other Mexican States. Rebellion in the Mexican states was harshly suppressed by Santa Anna causing thousands of victims among the civilian population.

7. There were many deaths among defenders and attackers in the Alamo. The surviving Alamo defenders were killed. Santa Anna also ordered the massacre of the Goliad prisoners who had been promised amnesty by General Urrea.

8. Following the Alamo and Goliad battles the cry "Remember the Alamo" was used as a battle cry to encourage the Texans to fight.

9. The same cry "Remember the Alamo" was used, after independence to excuse violence against the same Tejanos who supported independence. White Texans, abused, robbed, assassinated and lynched Tejanos, Mexicans and Mexican-Americans. Utilizing sheriffs, and Texas Rangers, they terrorized Tejanos, Mexican Americans and Mexicans into submission and to force them to abandon or sell lands and cattle for cheap. "Remember the Alamo" was used against Tejanos and Mexicans without distinction or reason. During the invasion of Mexico, the Texas Rangers plundered, abused and assassinated civilian Mexican citizens in Matamoros, Camargo and Monterrey again yelling "Remember the Alamo." Their biggest source of pride was that they were called the "Texas Devils" Their behavior was so cruel and criminal attacking the civilians, that forced General Taylor to send the Rangers back to Texas

10. The same battle cry "Remember the Alamo" is utilized today not only as a celebration of Texas independence but also in a way against Mexican Americans and Mexicans. As such the battle cry is used to symbolize Anglo and white race su-

premacy and to encourage discriminatory feelings against Mexican Americans and Mexicans. THAT CANNOT AND SHOULD NOT STAND IN OUR COUNTRY.

History is written by the victorious. There is another history. This history can be written by those who fought valiantly for what they considered a worthwhile cause but lost. They eventually became victims of the unforgiving, cruel and vengeful, winning side. This is their history.

Mexico was a young country when it inherited New Spain after an independence struggle that lasted 12 long years.

New Spain reached from the border between Costa Rica and Panama in Central America to well into North America including what now are Texas, New Mexico, Arizona, California, Nevada, Utah and half of Colorado.

This huge inheritance was too vast for Mexico to control. In fact, Mexico never had control of most of the territory she lost to the United States. This land, like territories in Central America that was to be inherited by Mexico, was never truly part of Mexico. It was part of New Spain that Mexico had to lose for lack of resources and people to control it. California was too far from Mexico City and Mexico never had control of the state. Californios were rather independent people. California was coveted not only by the United States but also by England and even Russia. The only areas of New Spain north of the present Mexico border where there was some Mexican control was New Mexico and the Trans-Nueces river area that was part of the Mexican States of Tamaulipas and Coahuila.

Texas was dangerous to live in because of the aggressive Indian nations. It was also far from Mexico City and no Mexican seemed to want to live there except temporarily. Other Mexican inhabitants were Catholic missionaries and members of quasi-military settlements who were living in communities isolated from one another. The civil government in San Antonio was established by immigrants from the Canarias (Canary) islands sent by the Spanish King in 1731. By 1836 the year of the Texas independence it is estimated that 3,600 or so Tejanos (Mexican Texans) lived in Texas which was part of the Mexican state of Coahuila-Texas. Texas never included the so-called Trans-Nueces Texas strip that include portions of the Mexican states of Tamaulipas and Coahuila (the area between the Nueces River and the Rio Grande).

The Mexican Government wanting to populate Texas to ensure control of the territory. To that purpose Mexican Governments invited Europeans and Americans to immigrate into Texas, assigning those who agreed, large tracts of land. Conditions to allow those immigrants the permit to move to Texas were, that they would swear allegiance to Mexico, learn Spanish, became Catholics and would renounce slavery. Several large concessions (Colonias) were stablished. Except for few individuals at the beginning of the deal, notably, Steven F Austin, most colonists never actually complied with the conditions to which they had agreed to be able to immigrate to Texas. Austin even fought on the Mexican army against an early (Fredonia) insurrection. Austin tried to convince the government to make several changes in the government of Texas. Because of that he was imprisoned for rebellion in Mexico City but later released. When he came back to Texas, he was ready for an independent Texas

Mexico's plans to populate Texas were conceptually good. If the plan would have been carried out as envisioned, Mexico would have had a "hard" border area. The area would have been populated by hardy European and American immigrants that would have made the United States think more than once before invading. The problem with the plan was that Mexico was a young, immature nation. Mexico was governed mostly by inexperienced, ambitious and corrupt individuals. Every individual who acquired a certain economic or political stature by whatever means, thought and was convinced that he could govern better than the current sitting president. Because of this Mexico experienced, nearly continuous revolution for the first one hundred plus year of independence.

In time, many unauthorized people moved into Texas. Often these new settlers were men of undesirable character, marauders, drunkards, and violent ruffians. Immigrants eventually outnumber Mexican descendants somewhere between twenty or twenty-five to one and with the gap increasing rapidly. The new settlers included General Sam Houston who led a double life., and was frequently drunk. Houston had military experience having fought in the war of 1812 where he impressed General Andrew Jackson with his ability, He had lived among Indian tribes in his younger years giving him significant knowledge of the Indian way of life. He separated from his first wife shorty and fled despondent to Arkansas territory to live among Indians. Here he married another woman. He never divorced his first wife until the Republic of Texas granted him an official divorce. He came to Texas as a land speculator and as a representative for Indian peace efforts.

Mexico had a turbulent history at the time of the Texas uprising. The country actually did not achieve internal peace until the late 1930s. Hundred years of unrest that included thirty years of dictatorship but relative peace by president (Dictator) Porfirio Diaz.

At the time of Texas independence and actually the cause of the independence itself was the unrest throughout Mexico caused by the abrogation of the Mexican Federal constitution of 1824. That constitution was patterned after the United States Constitution. Many Mexican states rebelled, including Zacatecas, where Santa Anna was particularly cruel, killing thousands of civilian Mexican citizens and punishing the state by taking territory to form another state.

The Texas rebellion against the new Centrist constitution that was to supersede the Federal constitution was supported not only by Texians (American Texans} but by Tejanos (Mexican Texans) and both fought against Santa Annas Forces. The flag flying at the Alamo was the tricolor Mexican Constitutionalist flag of 1824. Many Texans and Tejanos died in the Alamo and Goliad.in the ensuing battles.

Many fantasies are said about the Alamo battle that are directed not only against Santa Anna's forces but portrait Mexicans and Mexican Americans as criminals. The truth is there only was one cruel person in this story. And that is the criminal person of Santa Anna. He alone ordered the killing of the Alamo defendants and the defendants in Goliad. The Goliad defendants had been promised amnesty by General Urrea who actually took the fort. Santa Anna overruled Urrea's promise and when Urrea refused Santa Annas orders, Santa Anna send Lt. Col. De la Portilla from San Antonio to carry out the Goliad massacre.

Many Mexican soldiers died at the Alamo and many more at the San Jacinto battle, that occurred later on. The Mexican soldiers were just soldiers doing what soldiers do, fighting for their country. The Mexican soldiers were also heroic in the Alamo assault. Many of the Mexican loses there, were because Santa Anna did not wait a few days, when cannons would have arrived and had made the Alamo walls useless. Mexican soldiers, contrary to the popular belief, were poor Mexicans many of whom were conscripted by force and by commuted jail sentences. They we poorly dressed and poorly supplied. They were also forced to march with inadequate transportation, inadequate provisions and inadequate supplies. They were ill prepared for the inclement weather of the area. Many soldiers had died of exposure before crossing the Rio Grande due to a winter storm in Northern Mexico.

Santa Anna believed himself to be the Napoleon of the west. In reality he was an over-confident, arrogant individual, lacking strategic skills, good sense and maturity in his decisions. His actions were impulsive and capricious. When pursing the Texans into what ended in the San Jacinto Battle, he did so, taking only a small part of the available army. He was trusting his presumed great military abilities unequal in the western world. Afterall he was he thought, the Napoleon of the west. In many other battels particularly during the U.S. -Mexico war he made stupid mistakes leading to defeats rather than victories in battle.

Santa Annas cruelty began early, when he was a young Spanish military. In the battle of Medina, the single most lethal battle in Texas, he participated in the killing of large number of not only defenseless combatants but also in civilian reprisals.

Tejanos were part of the battle for independence of Texas but the Texans turned against them and treated them as the defeated enemy. They forced them to sell or abandon their properties. They used the Texas Rangers to terrorize Tejanos and Mexican ranch owners.

With the cry of "Remember the Alamo" The Texas Rangers killed, hung, and terrorized Mexican Americans living in the Trans Nueces strip. They forced Mexican American land owners to abandon them. They were the enforcers along with local police of the claim of racial superiority that forced Mexicans into practical servitude.

There are two outstanding symbols of the Texans Anglos hate against Mexicans and Tejanos of yesterday and today; The cry "Remember the Alamo "and the Texas Rangers who prided themselves in the killing and torturous treatment of Mexican Americans and Mexicans. It is high time that Anglos as well as ill-informed Americans in general stop being excited against Mexicans, Mexican Heritage and Texans of Mexican descent by distorted and falsely glorified historical tales and impressions.

Indeed, there were many Heroic and Glorious actions in the prelude, the actual actions and the aftermath of the battle of the Alamo. There were also many inglorious and barbaric acts. Both participants could take credit for them.

The Alamo should be remembered because it was this battle that gave origin to Texas independence. But is not and should not be a pretext to inflame hate against Mexican American and Mexicans.

Mexican Americans must be contented and happy with the outcome of the tumultuous relations between the two countries. The fact that Mexico's inability to hold onto the Spanish inheritance, resulted, by becoming American, the source of the United States' strength and world power. Mexico could not possibly keep that land and the risk is that that area of New Spain could have been British, French or even Russian

Now is up to us to fight for our rights as Americans.

MEXICAN AMERICAN PRIDE
PRINCIPLE NUMBER 20

As a Mexican American, Hispanic and Latin American, I will be prepared to promote and improve relations with all the American nations with whom we share the western hemisphere.

 IN THIS SECTION WE WILL DISCUSS THE FOLLOWING ISSUES:

1. The Western hemisphere, the Americas is the home of 36 political entities that include in the majority English and Spanish-speaking nations. There are also Portuguese, French, Dutch and Danish speaking areas.

2. The United States, an American nation has shown from its beginning more affinity with European nations, giving preference to northern European nations and people.

3. Early in its existence and ever since, the United States has manifested disdain and maintained mostly negative, arrogant, and threatening relations with other nations in the western hemisphere mainly to the continental Latin nations.

4. The American theory of the "divine destiny" or "manifest destiny" of the United States and its corollary Monroe Doctrine dictated the supremacy attitude of the United States towards the rest of the American Nations and political entities.

5. The consequence of the self-proclaimed United States su-

premacist international attitude is its perceived right to intervene in the affairs of any other American nation to protect whatever national security or economic issues it considers unilaterally threatening.

6. The most significant actions of the United States as a result of these theories and pronouncements were 1) The war with Mexico where the United States acquired over half of the territory Mexico inherited from Spain and, 2) The war with Spain that gave relative independence to Cuba and netted Puerto Rico, The Philippines and Guam to the United States.

7. Another significant United States intervention involved the fomenting of revolution in Panama against Colombia that gave independence to Panama. It also gave the United States the right to take over construction of the Panama Canal and control the Panama Canal Zone for nearly a century.

8. The perceived communist threat gave the United States the "right" to covertly foment revolutions and uprisings in Central America and most prominently in Chile and Cuba

9. Several American presidents have tried to improve relations with the Latin American nations, most significantly although short lived was "the Good Neighbor policy." This was a policy of President Franklin D. Roosevelt's prior to and during the Second World War that proclaimed non-intervention in the affairs of other (American) countries. This effort was changed with the Truman presidency and thereafter because of the fear of a Communist take-over of a large area of the continent.

10. The actual status of Cuban-American relations are the most ridiculous and yet most significant remaining issue between the United States and any other American nation. This issue

can only be resolved with the support and perhaps the initiative of the Cuban American population.

11. The USMCA free trade treaty is a great example of how a positive and productive relation is possible between the United States and a Latin America nation. All Latin American nations are involved in multiple and multinational trade agreements. Unfortunately, the United States has displayed a Luke-warm response to any participation in such arrangements.

12. There is a "new neighbor" in the Americas. The new neighbor is China. China represents a real challenge and threat to the hegemony of the United States over the continent. The Chinese are rapidly extending their influence over the Americas, particularly in South and Central America, the Caribbean islands and small continental nations.

13. The United States must re-evaluate and re-calibrate its relations with Latin American and other nations in the western hemisphere. The Chinese incursion into the continent is different from previous rivals of the United States in Latin America. The Chinese are extending their influence through economic and apparently non-political; non-military means. They are offering help to Latin-American nations with infrastructure mainly in communications and in connection to their "Belt and Road Initiative" This initiative is intended to provide Latin American nations with access to world markets as well as between neighbor nations.

14. To combat the Chinese initiatives on the continent, the United States should improve relations with Latin-America and consider improving terrestrial transportation links. The Pan-American Highway project must be revived by closing the "Darien Gap." The United States easily has the technology and the economic means to do it. Other nations in the conti-

nent will benefit and perhaps cooperate in the financing of the project. A Pan- American railway system should be planned. Perhaps a railway cannot be easily constructed at this time but technology is evolving and that challenge could easily be met in the not too distant future. Terrestrial communications would allow truck and bus transport between all American nations. These land-based connections would make economic and people to people relations easier and more profitable, helping to raise the status of poor and developing nations.

15. The need for the United States to retain and maintain their status in the Americas offers a great opportunity to Mexican Americans and all Latin-Americans in the country. Fluency in Spanish and other Latin languages could facilitate becoming involved in what can be called the "Latin-American initiative." English speakers are quick learners and English is the dominant international language so maybe Spanish-speaking advantage will not be lasting. There is another advantage that Latin Americans may have, and that is the cultural and personal Latin common experiences, besides well cemented bilingual ability. To participate in this Latin American initiative University training in American studies seem an excellent portal to a challenging, exciting and profitable carrier.

The Western Hemisphere is home to thirty-six political subdivisions in the two continents, North America, and South America.

Twenty of these are primarily Latin American countries and eighteen are Spanish speaking: Mexico, Guatemala, El Salvador, Honduras, Nicaragua, Costa Rica, Panama, Cuba, Dominican Republic, Colombia, Venezuela, Ecuador, Peru, Bolivia, Paraguay, Chile, Argentina and Uruguay. One is Portuguese speaking: Brazil and one French speaking: Haiti.

There is one bilingual country, Canada, where both English and French are official languages. There is also a bilingual primarily English-speaking nation, the United States, where Spanish is the second more frequently spoken language.

There are twelve relatively new independent, primarily island or smaller continental countries, mostly English speakers: Belize, Jamaica, the Bahamas, Antigua and Barbuda, Dominica, Saint Lucia, Saint Vincent and the Grenadines, Barbados, Grenada, Trinidad and Tobago, Guyana and Suriname. Surinam is the exception where Dutch is the language spoken.

There are two additional entities, one being Greenland which is a semi-autonomous country within the Danish Kingdom. The other, French Guyana is actually a department of France.

In addition, there are several islands in the Caribbean Sea and in the Atlantic under French, Dutch, British and Danish possession.

The United States is an American nation. Since the beginning however, the United States has had more affinity to the European Nations. On the other hand, the United States from the beginning has failed to maintain good relations with the Latin American nations.

The United States sees itself as the rightful director of the destiny of other American nations by virtue of its self-anointed divine or manifest destiny. The self-proclaimed Monroe Doctrine prescribed that no other nation must have rights to any American land, opposing further European colonization in the western hemisphere. At the same time the doctrine gave the United States the right to intervene anywhere in the continent at will, whenever it considered necessary for its interest. Using that principle, the United States successfully won a war with Mexico that deprived Mexico of over 50% of her territory. The victory over Mexico gave a boost to the theory of American Divine Destiny and gave the United States the power to become the Superpower that is today.

Under the Monroe Doctrine the United States intervened in Cuba on the pretext of the sinking of the USS Maine warship in Cuban waters blaming Spain for the ship's destruction. This intervention gave partial freedom to Cuba under protection and supervision of the United States. The War with Spain netted to the United States: Puerto Rico, Philippines, and Guam giving the United States a colonial Empire.

Using their assumed manifest destiny and the Monroe doctrine the United States invaded temporarily several American countries in Central America and the Caribbean. Later in the twentieth century, the United States covertly intervened in Chile. The intervention in Chile supported the overthrow of a democratically elected government and the installation of a military dictatorship, that of General Augusto Pinochet and his military junta. Pinochet was responsible for thousands of illegal arrests and civilian deaths as well as the disappearance of many citizens. Despite his many wrongdoings Chilean governments failed to convict him of any crimes. To date his crimes still pain the Chilean People; The failure to bring him to justice and make him pay for his crimes was and is the subject of national recriminations.

Up to now in the twentieth-first century there have been no significant challenges to the United States and its Monroe Doctrine with its hegemonic principles of manifest destiny. However, several times European nations have acted against American nations with the approval of the United States. In the case of Argentina trying to recover the Malvinas Islands (Falkland Islands) from Britain, the United States actually helped Britain to defeat Argentina militarily. Sovereignty over the islands have been disputed since the late 1700. The first settlement in the islands was built by the French who later left them in Spain possession. Britain never gave up claim to the islands. When Argentina became independent from Spain, it laid claim to the Islands. After several attempts at negotiating with Britain in 1982 Argentina invaded. Their possession lasted a few months until the British with a larger force, supported by the United States retook the Falklands. Argentina has not ceased to renew her claim to the Malvinas.

In the past, several United States' presidents have tried to improve relations with Latin America. The first positive approach, although short lived was initiated by President Franklin D Roosevelt when first elected. This initiative was entitled The Good Neighbor. The policy aimed to improve relations with Latin America at a time when there was increased international unrest prior to the Second World War. The United States seemed willing to correct its past imperialistic attitude towards Latin

America. Roosevelt's peaceful and progressive agenda endorsed the Pan-American resolution that proclaimed, "No country has the right to intervene in the internal or external affairs of another country." The Roosevelt policy assured the cooperation of most Latin American countries for most of the duration of the Second World War. Unfortunately, the good will implied in Roosevelt's Good Neighbor policy soon was forgotten under Truman and the presidents who followed him who were fearful of the communism threat.

The Cold War that pitted the United States and the USSR against each other brought unrest and conflict to the American continent. The United States saw those conflicts as a consequence of the rise of communism. President Truman helped Greece and Turkey with military and economic assistance. Truman then turned to Latin America and in order to fight the perceived communist threat, The United States fomented uprisings and conflicts by proxy in Central America and other nations. Some of the consequences of those interventions, poverty, crime, government abuse of human rights, and lack of security for individuals and families persist today in the year 2020.

The single greatest communist threat was brought about by the Cuban revolution led by Fidel Castro against the corrupt and abusive Batista regimen supported by the United States. The Cuban revolution ended when Batista left Cuba. The revolution was aided by multiple groups in Cuba fighting Batista but Fidel Castro seemed to be the unifying force. After Castro took over, he nationalized most of the American banks and industry in Cuba. In response Eisenhower cut diplomatic relations and communications with Cuba imposing an embargo. When Kennedy became president there were some efforts at negotiation but the Kennedy assassination ended any possible re-rapprochement. In return for Russian support and relief from the American embargo Cuba and Castro became involved in fomenting revolutions in Africa and Latin America including Cuban troops deployment.

Russian support to Cuba, was punctuated by the Russians placement of nuclear armaments in Cuban soil. The Russian move brought the world the menace of a nuclear conflict that only after some anxious moments was settled. The after-effects of the Cuban revolution and the United States' response to it persists to this day. It has been documented that there were multiple CIA. attempts to assassinate Fidel Castro. There was an attempted rapprochement during the Obama administration but Trump re-imposed the hardline American policy towards Cuba when he succeeded President Obama.

It is very difficult to justify the American policy towards Cuba which has lasted over sixty years. It seems that the United States would prefer a Cuba led by a legitimate and democratic government and not a Bautista type, corrupt one. Negotiation with the current revolutionary regime if well intentioned could result in the establishment of a Democratically elected government. The United States has good relations with recent with former enemies from previous conflicts. It makes no sense then that relations with a neighbor small American country cannot be made to work. The Cuban people living in the island nation deserve a respite. The Cuban people living in the United States need to allow themselves to love their native country. They should know by now, that the politicians who falsely promise to give them back their former privileged life in Cuba are just playing a political game. The Republicans keep using the Cuban Americans desire for a return to the old Cuba in order to win their votes. The United States has no hurry in even attempting to negotiate with Cuba under Republicans administrations, happy to use the Cubans hopes. The Republican ploy is the same as Democrats use with Mexican Americans playing with their hope of support for Mexican Americans important issues. Only the Cuban Americans of today can help the impoverished Cubans left in the island. They can help them by showing them that Cubans can make it anywhere. Cuban Americans have made a paradise of the state of Florida. Formerly decaying Miami and southern Florida are now a rich, beautiful part of the country. That is an example of Cuban Americans effort. It is an example of what Cuban Americans can do. Cuban Americans are without doubt the most accomplished Hispanic American group in this country. Cuban Americans themselves should led a rapprochement with confidence and good faith. Maybe the Organization of American States (OAS) can help. It is very much in the interest of the OAS that this estate of conflict be resolved.

The resolution of the Cuba situation would go a long way to changing the Latin American feeling that the United States does not care about Latin America. The persistent opinion among American presidents and the American public opinion is that Latin American countries and Latin American peoples are not worth much. Examples of such opinions are abundant but there is no need to repeat those inflammatory statements here. What we need to concentrate now is to make Americans realize that Latin American nations are important to the United States economically and in security matters.

By now the benefits of the North America Free trade agreement (NAFTA) and its successor, The United States Mexico Canada (USMCA) free trade agreement, are readily apparent in the three participating countries. Trade between the countries increased fourfold. Employment increased reaching the lowest unemployment rate in the United States in the year 2020. A temporary increase in unemployment prior to the time was because of migration of industry to China and not to Mexico. The gross national product of the three nations increased. Industries such as the auto industry of the United States benefited. Many American cars are produced in Mexico but thanks to the Mexican trade arrangements with over fifty countries the American cars are exported to those countries with much of the benefit coming back to companies in the United States. Agricultural product export and import benefited. For example, the greater productivity of the highly mechanized American agriculture exported great amounts to Mexico. Conversely the small farm of Mexican Agricultural exports to the United States rocketed. The consumer in both counties benefited by lower prices and agricultural product variety. The increased commercial and industrial activity in Mexico allowed many of the former Mexican undocumented migrants to the United States stay home. This effect was so great that more Mexicans came back to Mexico than Mexicans left to the United States. Even today many Mexicans who migrated legally to the United

States and even became American citizens are coming back to Mexico to enjoy new opportunities.

Because of the increased commercial traffic between Mexico, the United States, and Canada, these countries have become the most important import and export partners to each other. The increased commerce has been particularly important to the border states, Texas, California, Michigan and Arizona but it seems that most American states have benefited. On the other hand, Canada has received some important benefits, enjoying export products to the United States and Mexico. For Mexico the magnitude of the North American traffic is a lifeline. Without this lifeline Mexico would be a much poorer country, its citizens would have to become illegal immigrants to survive, as in the past.

Hispanics have become the majority minority in the country and seemingly are in the way to become the majority of the population in several states such as Texas and California. Latent and tentative Mexican American political power is building, but it is limited by the unwillingness of Mexican Americans to participate in the electoral process. When Mexican Americans wake up and fulfill their duty as American citizens their importance and power to change American perceptions and behavior will be evident. One of the changes we have to make in American perceptions is to help them wake up to the importance of Latin American countries and peoples to the United States. Hopefully that awakening will occur before other countries, for now, China wins the trust and benefits of Latin America commerce and friendship. Mexican Americans and other Latin American groups must undertake the opportunity and unspoken duty to enlighten white Americans about the need and opportunity to improve relations with Latin American nations. All the western hemisphere nations are very much dependent of the United States to partner with any American nation that need its assistance. They need a willing leader and partner badly, but they do not need a big nation meddling in their internal affairs and taking advantage of its size and power. They do not need the "America First and you do whatever I allow you to do" ideology that Trump represents.

The land area of South America is nearly twice the area of the continental United States and its population is 430 million people. Central America is approximately fifteen times smaller than the continental United States and has 49 million inhabitants. That represents 480 million of possible clients and partners available to an open American economy. Including the population of Canada, Mexico and the Caribbean nations the number that could participate in a group led by the United States is over 660 million people. In other words, altogether they could form an economic union of one billion people when the population of the United States is included. To take full advantage of the economic potential of the American nations there has to be a willingness of the most advanced members of the group Canada, Mexico, Brazil, Chile, Argentina, Peru, and Colombia to commit to helping the others to improve their economy and of course the leadership and help of the United States.

All of us, Mexican Americans, Cuban Americans, Puerto Rican Americans and other Latin Americans need to get involved in the process of uniting the continent with a shared commitment to Progress and Justice. All of us have to become ambassadors for the American nations. Of course, all non-Latin Americans and Canadians are welcome and indeed are required for the dream to succeed. Mexican Americans and Latin Americans should take advantage of the involvement in the Pan-American progress because of the common language. However, involvement and enthusiasm of non-Latin Americans may be key to the success of this effort.

North and South America offer varied and rich natural resources that could provide great mutual benefits to the nations of the two continents. This is of course in addition to the potential of vast human resources that could be better utilized. For this to occur strategic planning is needed. Education, social programs to redeem the poorest inhabitants and guided exploitation of natural and human resources are needed. Also needed is free commerce, appropriate industrial activity and appropriate governmental programs. There is evidence that some of these priority changes are occurring having been stimulated by international commerce in South America. The USMCA agreement has provided clarity about what each of the three nations in North America can do better in each sphere of their commercial activities. The mutual free trade agreement in South America Mercosur, is defining what each South American nation can do better than its neighbors. The South American nations are learning rapidly what they need to succeed in international commercial relations. Commercial initiatives with the European Union are being negotiated. Mexico-Brazil and Mexico- Mercosur relations are active, as is the Pacific Alliance of Free Trade between Mexico, Colombia, Peru and Chile. The Comprehensive and Progressive Agreement on Trans-Pacific Partnership, which consists of remnants of the Trans Pacific Partnership from which the United States withdrew, links eleven nations and other international commercial treaties. This new partnership agreement is teaching South American nations about organization and commercial success. Most of these treaties are being activated without the United States' participation.

It is not possible to quantify what the lack of involvement from the United States in all of these international treaties signify. The United States economy is so large and the strength of the American dollar is so-great that maybe there is no significant damage to the United States. Under Trump, the binational treaties that the United States prefers over multinational treaties may provide equal benefits to the United States. Without the compromises needed in a multinational treaty the United States can set more coercive conditions. The coercive conditions of the America First policy are possible because of the monetary, economic and military might of the United States. The American economic and military might dictate an international behavior under Trump that is less accommodating than traditional American leadership. This new behavior emphasizes might, versus traditional diplomacy. The Trump policy can be seen as a whole world extension of the "Manifest Destiny" of the United States.

One of the barriers to better relations with Latin America is lack of a terrestrial transport network. There is no good substitute for highway and railroad shipping. Air and oceanic transportation are more expensive, less flexible and more complex than terrestrial transport. Terrestrial transportation is able to make as many stops and starts as needed to pick-up and deliver goods services and people. Terrestrial transportation facilitates intra-national and international commerce. Trucks and buses on highways and railroad transport are flexible and efficient.

In the 1930s and 1940s the idea of a Pan-American highway was considered. In fact, the Pan-American Highway exists today. The Pan American Highway starts in Alaska and ends in Southern Argentina or Southern Chile. It has alternative routes that can cover every continental American country. There is only one problem in the continuity of this highway and it is the Darien Gap. The Darien area is a sixty mile stretch of inhospitable impassable jungle, marshy watershed and mountain. Attempts have been made to construct a highway through it without success. Completing this gap in the Pan American highway is not so much impossible as it is expensive. A highway built on pylons as Interstate Highway 10 in Louisiana would accomplish it. While completing the Pan-American Highway why not begin to plan for an Inter- American rail system? It may not be possible at this time but why not in the future?

Highway and railroad communications in South America are difficult. The greatest difficulty is represented by the high and wide Andes Mountain range. With the help of China, a trans- Andean railroad is being constructed between Peru and Bolivia. A second trans-Andean project links Bolivia with the Pacific Ocean in Chile. Similar projects link Argentina, Uruguay, Brazil and Bolivia. Yet another project links Peru, Ecuador, Colombia, and Venezuela and extends through Guyana, Surinam, French Guyana and back to Brazil. Some of these projects are part of the Chinese Belt and Road initiative. Incidentally an antenna built in southernmost Argentina is part of China's plans to land a vehicle in the dark side of the moon.

The involvement of China in commerce and as a transportation facilitator represents a significant challenge to the United States. China has expanded South-American trade, bailed out governments, insured access to enormous natural resources and increased military ties. China is now the second most important commercial partner to South America. China also shares projects in Central America significantly in the Panama Canal but also in El Salvador and the Caribbean. China is challenging American domination of Latin America. It may be important for Latin American countries that China does not aim for political hegemony, they seem to care only for economic relations and dominance. That is for money issues, by improving those countries' economies, China shares economic gains. Their behavior in South America is not different to that of ethnic Chinese in south Asia: Vietnam, Philippines, Indonesia, etc. For that matter, the Chinese involvement in the United States scientific and economic matters fits perfectly with Chinese behavior elsewhere. Incidentally China is now involved in Greenland as a Belt and Road Initiative member.

Mexican Americans, Latin Americans, and all United States citizens would benefit from studies that prepare them to act as representatives of the United States in Latin America. In turn they would also become good will ambassadors for Latin American countries. Study on Latin American relations and Canada are available in many universities. One particularly promising program will be offered at the University of the Incarnate Word (UIW) in San Antonio, Texas. Their Institute of The Americas will promote better understanding and stronger relations with Mexico, Central and South America, and Canada. Anyone, and particularly any Mexican American, who registers for the American studies program, at UIW could be embarking on a productive challenging and fulfilling career.

EPILOGUE:
A MEXICAN AMERICAN DREAM

 I DREAM OF THE DAY:

when Mexican Americans go to work in a safe environment without fear for themselves or their family;

when they are treated fairly and paid living wages;

when our farmworkers and low-skilled workers are respected and their work appreciated;

when the children of low-skilled workers are given access to good education and the ability to succeed in higher-paid occupations;

when all Mexican American students graduate from the highest studies they choose as their objective;

when our workers become leaders and are recognized with promotion and higher responsibility in their workplace;

when Mexican American parents become role models to their families and guide their children and extended family on the ways to succeed;

when all our people have access to good health services and choose healthy lifestyles;

when we support our fellow Mexican Americans in their efforts to succeed in life and livelihood;

when all our people choose excellence as their objective;

when we support the Mexican American organizations that support us;

when no enterprise, business, or organization denigrates or discriminates against Mexican Americans;

when we visibly contribute to our country's prominence and leadership in the world;

when all Mexican Americans feel they belong and are valued as citizens of the United States;

when all Mexican Americans vote and, as any American citizen, elect the representative of their choice;

when all of us come to the defense of any Mexican American who is attacked, injured, oppressed, hurt, or killed because of his or her ethnicity;

and when Mexican Americans are truly guaranteed the unalienable rights of equality, justice, and the pursuit of happiness.

This is our Mexican American dream; I hope, having read this book, you recognize your own in it and we can work separately and together to improve the lives and the status of Mexican Americans in this great country. No one but ourselves will realize our dreams for us. Each one of us has work to do, to attain a better life for the Mexican American people in America. But our time has arrived. The twenty chapters of this book offer descriptions of the work needed to become outstanding American citizens.

Don't be daunted; everything suggested is achievable,
for we have a vision and a dream…

www.ingramcontent.com/pod-product-compliance
Lightning Source LLC
Chambersburg PA
CBHW070657250726
48662CB00001B/160